EXPERIENCING
the
SPIRIT

EXPERIENCING
the
SPIRIT

The Power of Pentecost Every Day

HENRY & MELVIN
BLACKABY

MULTNOMAH
BOOKS

EXPERIENCING THE SPIRIT
PUBLISHED BY MULTNOMAH BOOKS
12265 Oracle Boulevard, Suite 200
Colorado Springs, Colorado 80921

ISBN 978-1-59052-911-9
ISBN 978-1-60142-175-3 (e-book)

Published in the United States by WaterBrook Multnomah, an imprint of The Crown Publishing Group, a division of Random House Inc., New York.

MULTNOMAH and its mountain colophon are registered trademarks of Random House Inc.

Library of Congress Cataloging-in-Publication Data
Blackaby, Henry T., 1935–
    Experiencing the spirit : the power of Pentecost every day / Henry Blackaby and Mel Blackaby. — 1st ed.
        p. cm.
    ISBN 978-1-59052-911-9
    1. Holy Spirit. 2. Christian life. I. Blackaby, Melvin D. II. Title.
    BT121.3.B54 2009
    231'.3—dc22

                                    2008044042

Printed in the United States of America
2011

10 9 8 7 6 5

SPECIAL SALES
Most WaterBrook Multnomah books are available in special quantity discounts when purchased in bulk by corporations, organizations, and special interest groups.
Custom imprinting or excerpting can also be done to fit special needs. For information, please e-mail SpecialMarkets@WaterBrookMultnomah.com or call 1-800-603-7051.

CONTENTS

GOD'S EXCLAMATION POINT

Jesus stood and cried out, saying, "If anyone thirsts, let him come to Me and drink. He who believes in Me, as the Scripture has said, out of his heart will flow rivers of living water." But this He spoke concerning the Spirit, whom those believing in Him would receive; for the Holy Spirit was not yet given, because Jesus was not yet glorified.

—JOHN 7:37–39

When it comes to the work of the Holy Spirit in the believer's life, few topics have been so popular and so neglected at the same time. It's a popular topic because people want power; they want to experience something of the divine in their life, something beyond their normal human experience, and the Holy Spirit seems to be the easy ticket. And whereas Jesus is clearly established in his authoritative role as Lord, there's a misconception that the Spirit can be readily manipulated. Because He's called the Comforter, Helper, or Counselor, many Christians assume that the Spirit's purpose is to be our servant and help us enjoy abundant life. But that view is fundamentally inadequate. Jesus sent the Spirit not for us, but for *Him*— to carry out His rule and authority in our lives.

Too often, we fall into a self-centered approach to our walk with God that emphasizes what *we* get out of it, what *we* can experience if we're filled with the Spirit. We neglect the biblical teaching that clearly describes the Spirit's role in our lives and what God wants us to experience. But when we finally understand our relationship with the Holy Spirit, we'll then truly experience a transformed life in step with the purposes of God.

THE PINNACLE OF CHRIST'S WORK

As we consider the impact of Pentecost and the gift of the Holy Spirit to everyone who believes, we must first keep this topic in context. Think of Christ's work in three distinct yet unified stages: the Cross, the Resurrection, and the gift of Pentecost. All three are significant in their own way but must be understood together as a unified whole.

At the Cross, the power of sin and its consequences were dealt a deathblow. Whereas sin once had power over us, now we've been given power over sin. As Paul said, "The message of the cross is foolishness to those who are perishing, but to us who are being saved it is the power of God" (1 Corinthians 1:18). There should be no proliferation of sin among God's people, for in the Cross we've been given victory over sin.

Why then do God's people still live in sin? There are several reasons, but two stand out above the rest.

First, it's their choice. They've become content to live without the manifest power of God in their lives. Though they've been given all the power they need to overcome the Evil One, they enjoy sin too much to apply the power of the Cross that sets them free.

Second, they've never been fully and clearly taught the truth of God's Word. Though Satan has been defeated, he still has the power to deceive, and those who aren't grounded biblically are his easiest victims. As long as he keeps them from the truth, he can keep them in his imaginary chains.

But make no mistake: the Cross is sufficient. Christ paid the price to forever set us free from sin. Yet the story of the Cross is not the end. Whereas the Cross set us free from sin, the Resurrection gives us power to live a new life. The Resurrection is not another doctrine to believe, but a reality to experience. It is proof of Christ's victory over sin and our hope of salvation. Just as Christ was raised to new life, so we experience new life in Him, a new life that begins the day we accept Christ as our Lord and Savior.

This Resurrection reality brings you into a wholly different dimension that allows you to see and experience what others cannot. Jesus told His disciples, "It has been given to you to know the mysteries of the kingdom of heaven, but to them [those who aren't His disciples] it has not been given" (Matthew 13:11). Here again, many Christians don't understand—or haven't appropriated into their lives—the wonderful power of the Resurrection.

How about you? If you've been given ability to understand the mysteries of God, are you using your spiritual senses to detect God's activity and to adjust your life accordingly? Or do you act like the world, ignoring God until you need Him to bail you out of a crisis? The power of the Resurrection is a gift that must be opened and lived out. And with that gift, those who earnestly seek to live as children of God will walk with Him and experience His purposes in their lives.

The Cross and Resurrection are incredible events with far-reaching impact upon our lives. Yet without the gift of the Spirit at Pentecost, they're inaccessible to us. The pinnacle of Christ's work was to send the Holy Spirit to dwell in the heart of everyone who believes. For the Spirit takes Christ's work on the cross and through the Resurrection and brings that work to bear upon our lives. Thus He completes His work of salvation in our lives.

That's why *Experiencing the Spirit* is so important as the conclusion of a three-book series that includes *Experiencing the Cross* and *Experiencing the Resurrection.* All three events in the life of Jesus stand alone, but they find their intended purpose as a collective whole. This third book becomes, in a way, the exclamation point of all that God has done on your behalf. For the Spirit will bring you spiritual insight, practical application, and empowerment to live out the truth of God's great salvation day by day.

In this book we'll keep returning to various foundational truths about the Spirit from the Word of God, truths that the Lord has engraved on our hearts. We'll revisit them from various angles to help you more deeply reflect on them and respond to them. As the Holy Spirit of God causes your heart to embrace and obey these truths, and as they become more and more at home in your inner being, you'll never grow tired of hearing them and thanking God for them.

Where It All Started

Looking back to the church in the first century, we're amazed at the impact of a people who appear to have had inadequate resources for such a monumental task. There were no seminaries to train their pastors, no beautiful church buildings in which to worship, and no such thing as a Bible in every member's hand. They had no elaborate sound systems or multimedia tools at their disposal, no celebrities to endorse their cause, and hardly any freedom to promote their belief in Jesus Christ. For the most part, they were plain men and women, insignificant and unknown, fighting against fierce opposition and hatred. But Scripture testifies that they "turned the world upside down" (Acts 17:6). Wave after wave of persecution broke over them, yet they emerged victorious. The message of the early church, as told in the book of Acts, is that the bare simplicity of the Christian faith is what counts. The testimony of early Christians was that *God's people proclaimed the gospel in the power of the Holy Spirit and confirmed it with holy lives.*

So what's the secret? There is no secret. The Bible clearly tells us of a gift from God that unleashes the power and wisdom of His kingdom—providing "all things that pertain to life and godliness" (2 Peter 1:3). Jesus told the apostles not to leave Jerusalem, but to wait for this promised gift from the Father:

> John truly baptized with water, but you shall be baptized
> with the Holy Spirit not many days from now.... You shall
> receive power when the Holy Spirit has come upon you; and
> you shall be witnesses to Me in Jerusalem, and in all Judea
> and Samaria, and to the end of the earth. (Acts 1:5, 8)

The result of the Spirit's coming upon the apostles was beyond earthshaking; the Spirit-filled disciples literally shook the gates of hell. So dramatic was the coming of the Spirit upon the apostles that their enemies couldn't deny the power and wisdom they displayed: "Now when they saw the boldness of Peter and John, and perceived that they were uneducated and untrained men, they marveled" (Acts 4:13).

Does the world *marvel* at the church today? Unfortunately, much of what happens in the contemporary church is little more than a reflection of the values and the reasoning of the surrounding culture. When it comes to serving God, we tend to look at what we're good at and what we like to do, then serve according to our ability. The result: we don't need the Holy Spirit because we think we have everything under control. The world therefore sees good people doing good things for their God, but they don't see the power of God working through His people to accomplish what only He can do.

So here's a question: will God ever ask you to do something you're not able to do? The answer is yes—all the time! It *must* be that way, for God's glory and kingdom. If we function according to our ability alone, we get the glory; if we function according to the power of the Spirit within us, God gets the glory. He wants to reveal *Himself* to a watching world.

The purposes of God are based not on our ability, but upon His ability to work through us. Hence, the gift! The Holy Spirit is the indispensable gift God has given to every believer. As Peter proclaimed on the day of Pentecost, "Repent, and let every one of you be baptized in the name of Jesus Christ for the remission of sins; and *you shall receive the gift of the Holy Spirit*" (Acts 2:38).

GET READY

This book will reorient your thinking back to biblical teaching on the Spirit's role in your life. It will also clarify the apparent confusion between natural talents and spiritual gifts, and help you get in step with God's purpose for your life. As you understand the strategic plan in the heart of God to send the gift of the Holy Spirit, you won't struggle with burnout from serving God or carry the weight of anxiety and stress. Your Christian life will produce joy, not burdens that weigh heavy on your soul.

The gift of Pentecost was not just for the early believers; it's for you. As you study this book, you'll discover there are no excuses for watching the activity of God from a distance. He has chosen and equipped every believer for kingdom work.

God sent the Holy Spirit on assignment. So what is that assignment? What is He doing in your life? How do you get in step with Him and enjoy abundant life as Christ has promised? This book, though not an exhaustive study on the Holy Spirit, will be a practical guide to allowing the Spirit to help you experience the power of God's great salvation in every area of your life.

As you begin, we'd like you to consider a couple of issues.

First, *allow the Holy Spirit to open the Scriptures and teach you.* Too often we come to a study like this with a lot of baggage that may or may not be biblical. We allow many things to shape our thinking—past experiences, books we've read, teaching we've listened to, or just our own assumptions. So come with an open mind and heart to experience the fullness of the Spirit. Listen carefully to the Holy Spirit, for He's the Spirit of Truth.

Second, ask yourself some tough questions: *Can I honestly say I'm experiencing the power of the Holy Spirit in my life? If not, why not?*

The promise of God has been given you, and He expects your life to be shaped by His presence. You cannot remain the same. So prepare yourself to make some adjustments according to what the Spirit shows you.

PART ONE

Gift of the Spirit in the Heart and Mind of God

Chapter I

REVEALING THE UNKNOWABLE

*"Eye has not seen, nor ear heard, nor have entered into
the heart of man the things which God has prepared for
those who love Him." But God has revealed them to us
through His Spirit. For the Spirit searches all things,
yes, the deep things of God.*

—1 Corinthians 2:9–10

The person who does not know the Holy Spirit of God does not know God. It's that simple. It's true that God so loved the world that He gave His only begotten Son to provide eternal salvation and that, through His death and resurrection, we have victory over sin and new life in Christ. But apart from the Holy Spirit, God's great salvation is of no relevance to us. Apart from the active work of the Spirit in our lives, we would neither know God nor have the ability to respond to Him. Divine truth is not something we "discover"; it is revealed by the Holy Spirit of God. As such, no other reality in the Christian life is as important as being filled with the Spirit.

The doctrine of the Holy Spirit is distinctive to the Christian faith. No other religion has anything like it. What believers in Jesus Christ have come to know and experience through His gift of the Spirit brings them into a relationship with God that's inaccessible in all other religions of the world. For just as God did not create the world and then step back and watch it spin, but chose to enter time and space and interact with His people, so also God did not just deliver a set of laws for us to follow in the hope of earning our way to heaven. Instead He chose to enter a relationship with His people on earth through His indwelling Spirit.

Trapped in Attic Darkness

When I (Mel) was sixteen years old, I had a summer job as a laborer on a construction crew. My boss was a small contractor who built homes, but he also renovated older homes. One day he sent me to an old house to install pink Fiberglass insulation in the attic. The outdoor temperature that day reached 95 degrees Fahrenheit, so you can imagine how hot it was in that dusty old attic. I felt like I was working in a convection oven.

It was a nasty job. As I shone my flashlight around the attic, I saw a cloud of Fiberglass particles floating through the air. All day long I worked in that dark and dusty deathtrap. It was one of those labor jobs that encouraged me to later go back to school and get an education.

That night I was exhausted when my head hit the pillow. I guess the day's work had had an impact on me, because I had a nightmare about being trapped in the attic. I got up in the middle of the night in a cold sweat—yet I wasn't fully awake. I started to panic, thinking I was still in the attic and couldn't find my way out. I scrambled frantically around the room looking for the attic's crawl-out door and nearly destroyed my room in the process. I threw my dresser across the room and pulled down bookshelves. I was lost in the closet when suddenly a light shone through the crack under my door.

"Mel?" It was my mother's voice. "Is everything okay?"

Seeing the light, I got my bearings and knew exactly where I was and the reality of my situation. It was just a dream!

My mom opened the door and saw my demolition work. "What's going on?" she questioned.

"Oh, it's nothing... Just got a little disoriented."

I'd been in a nightmare I couldn't escape—trapped in darkness and unable to perceive reality—until the light was turned on. Only when a little light shone under the door did my situation become clear to me.

In the same way, unless the Holy Spirit turns the light on, your life will be kept in complete darkness, disoriented to the things of God. There's absolutely nothing you can do to find the light; you're at the complete mercy of God to reveal it. All you can perceive is what you see and experience in the physical world, but there's a spiritual reality to which you're blind.

SIN'S DAMAGE

Look at Paul's description in Romans 3 of sin's damage:

"There is none righteous, no, not one;
There is none who understands;
There is none who seeks after God.
They have all turned aside;
They have together become unprofitable;
There is none who does good, no, not one."
"Their throat is an open tomb;
With their tongues they have practiced
      deceit";
"The poison of asps is under their lips";
"Whose mouth is full of cursing and
      bitterness."
"Their feet are swift to shed blood;

Destruction and misery are in their ways;
And the way of peace they have not known.
There is no fear of God before their eyes."
   (verses 10–18)

Paul went on to say, "All have sinned and fall short of the glory of God" (verse 23). *Everyone* has fallen short; *everyone* has sinned. And sin has fatal consequences. Not only has it separated you from God, but it also keeps you from restoring that relationship.

Paul emphasized these points in Romans 3:

- Sin makes you unrighteous and separates you from God.
- Sin keeps you from understanding God.
- Sin keeps you from seeking God.
- Sin causes you to turn to other things, leaving you worthless and setting you on the road to depravity.
- Sin ultimately causes you to lose the fear of God. And when you lose the fear of God, there's no deterrent to sin; you can't stop your downward plunge into eternal destruction.

The reality of our spiritual state can look pretty depressing. Is there any hope? Many would answer no. Some have committed suicide. Many more have attempted suicide, and even more have contemplated it.

One of the most influential opponents of Christianity was Friedrich Nietzsche, who called Christianity "the one great curse" and "the one immortal blemish of mankind." He proclaimed "the death of God" as a cultural fact and claimed atheism as the last evolutionary phase in the search for truth. Nietzsche later was debilitated by mental illness; having no hope, he'd gone mad.

If not for the grace of God, we all would be in the same condition—without hope. For we have all sinned, and sin prevents a relationship with God—and life apart from God leaves no hope.

Proof of God at Work

But if you find yourself experiencing a desire to seek God, we have great news for you: *God is already at work in you.* The fact that you're searching for Him is an indication that God is pursuing you and drawing you into a relationship with Him that's real and personal. Apart from His active work in your life, you would never have the desire to seek Him. For as we've seen, because of sin, "There is none who understands; there is none who seeks after God" (Romans 3:11).

Theologians use the term *prevenient grace* to describe God's work of drawing us to Himself. Before we in our fallen state can seek God, He must first create the desire within us for spiritual realities. There must be a work of enlightenment done within us before we're aware of our need for salvation. That's why we believe no one can go to church or open God's Word "by accident." God is drawing them, whether or not they realize it. If you find yourself wanting to consider spiritual truth, it's not because of some funny feeling, but because God Himself draws you.

King David showed us something about this when he cried out to God, "My soul clings to You; Your right hand upholds me" (Psalm 63:8, NASB). When we reach out to cling to Him, it's God who is drawing us, and it's God who holds us there. There's no contradiction in this divine upholding and human following. For our part, there must be a response to God's drawing power if we're to experience a relationship with Him.

It's like a man trying to draw a woman's affection; the relationship will not blossom unless the woman responds. And when you *do* respond to God's leading, He will give you the ability to answer the call. As James told us, "Draw near to God and He will draw near to you" (4:8).

Listen carefully: *Recognizing God* is not the same as coming to Him. *Hearing God* in your heart is not the same as answering. *Working for the kingdom of God* does not mean living in the kingdom of God. Christianity is not believing the truths of the Bible; it's *acting* upon them and allowing God control of your life. You must *respond* to God and make the choice to interact personally with Him.

Have you gone beyond accepting the fact that there's a God? Have you moved beyond accepting Christ as God's Son and made Him Lord of your life? If you believe there's a God, that He sent His

Son to die for you, that God raised Jesus from the dead after three days, and that Christ is coming back for His disciples—that's great. But Satan also believes all that! What makes your life any different from Satan's? To be different, you must come to Christ, pursue Him, give your life to Him, and keep growing in your relationship with Him—*for He's a Person to be loved, not an idea to be accepted.*

No Longer Dormant

All that we've been talking about is the active work of the Holy Spirit in your life. If God had not sent the Holy Spirit to open your eyes, you wouldn't see Him. If the Holy Spirit hadn't opened your ears, you wouldn't hear Him. If the Holy Spirit hadn't touched your heart, you wouldn't have the slightest desire to know Him.

We've all been taught that we have five senses—sight, smell, taste, hearing, and touch. By using them, we can apprehend most realities. But when it comes to apprehending God, we struggle. We don't see Him, smell Him, taste Him, hear Him, or touch Him. But there is within us another sense by which we can know God as certainly as we know material things by our five familiar senses. Because we're spiritual creatures created in the image of God (Genesis 1:26), we have spiritual faculties that allow us to truly know Him. We can apprehend Him; we can experience Him; we can love Him.

In non-Christians, this faculty lies dormant. It's asleep in their nature. For all practical purposes it is dead because of sin. But this faculty is quickened to life by the work of the Holy Spirit when we're born again.

The sending of the Spirit was part of God's plan from the beginning, and that plan was fulfilled on the Day of Pentecost. In fact, the sermon delivered by Peter that day was focused primarily on God the Father working in and through the life of His Son, Jesus. This brief selection from that sermon shows Peter's emphasis:

> Men of Israel, hear these words: Jesus of Nazareth, a Man attested by *God* to you by miracles, wonders, and signs which *God* did through Him in your midst, as you yourselves also know—Him, being delivered by the determined purpose and foreknowledge of *God,* you have taken by lawless hands, have crucified, and put to death; whom *God* raised up, having loosed the pains of death, because it was not possible that He should be held by it. (Acts 2:22–24)

Notice that God the Father was the one who orchestrated the events in the life of Jesus. In the same way, the Father brought forth the dramatic coming of the Spirit on the Day of Pentecost. It's true that Jesus sent the Spirit, but only after He had "received from the Father the promise of the Holy Spirit" (Acts 2:33). So we see that the coming of the Holy Spirit was in the heart of God from the very beginning.

Furthermore, the text of Peter's sermon that day was from the Old Testament prophet Joel. Peter said,

> But this is what was spoken by the prophet Joel:
> "And it shall come to pass in the last days,
>   says God,
> That I will pour out of My Spirit on all
>   flesh;
> Your sons and your daughters shall
>   prophesy,
> Your young men shall see visions,
> Your old men shall dream dreams."
>   (Acts 2:16–17; see Joel 2:28)

Long before Jesus arrived in the flesh, God the Father was talking about this day. It was always planned as the next significant event after Jesus died and rose again—as *the* necessary event to bring the work of Christ to bear upon those who would believe.

Why then do many Christians fail to experience the depths of what God has purposed for their lives? The reason is their insufficient personal dealing with God. When our faith is based primarily on the wisdom of men and not on the power of God, we've just nullified most of what God intended for our lives. When our faith is built only on a collection of doctrines, we miss out on the Person who wants to be our life.

Like all personal relationships, this spiritual relationship is activated through faith. When faith is defective, the result is numbness toward spiritual things. Some have never given their whole heart to God yet wonder why they haven't experienced Him. To live the Christian life in its fullness, you must have faith. "The just shall live by faith" (Romans 1:17), Paul said, and in Hebrews we read, "Without faith it is impossible to please [God]" (Hebrews 11:6). You must take God at His word! Every positive response to the Lord will open up new opportunities to know Him more and more. The more you pursue Him, the more He'll reveal Himself to you.

WIND IN THE SAILS

To get a picture of the Spirit, consider the image of a sailing ship. The sailors make sure everything's ready to go. The decks are swabbed, the trim freshly painted, and the galley stocked with food for the voyage. The anchor's up, the ropes are in, the sails are raised, and the captain's at the helm.

But the ship doesn't move.

Why? Because the sails need wind to propel the ship forward.

You can prepare everything in your life to go forward with God, but without the wind of the Spirit, there's no movement. On a sailing ship you're at the mercy of nature and the necessary wind to move; in life, you're at the mercy of God and the Spirit's power. Without that power, we can't follow God and experience life to its fullest.

Interestingly, the Greek and Hebrew words for Spirit (*pneuma* and *ruah*) can both be translated as "wind" or "breath." Unless the wind of the Spirit blows, you'll drift aimlessly along on the currents of life. Even after you've done everything you know to connect with God, it's all in vain without action on His part.

With this in mind, can you understand why "blasphemy against the Spirit" is so serious? Look at the amazing and even terrifying statement about this from Jesus:

> Therefore I say to you, every sin and blasphemy will be forgiven men, but the blasphemy against the Spirit will not be forgiven men. Anyone who speaks a word against the Son of Man, it will be forgiven him; but whoever speaks against the Holy Spirit, it will not be forgiven him, either in this age or in the age to come. (Matthew 12:31–32)

Why would Jesus make such a statement? Why is it more dangerous to speak against the Holy Spirit than to speak against the Son of Man, Jesus Himself? Simply this: the Holy Spirit is the only one who moves upon a person to bring conviction of sin and the desire to be in a right relationship with God. Speaking of the Holy Spirit, Jesus said, "When He has come, He will convict the world of sin, and of righteousness, and of judgment" (John 16:8). Without this work of the Spirit, you're incapable of responding to God.

So the Holy Spirit is not to be ignored or taken for granted. He's not to be cast aside as insignificant in comparison to God the Father and God the Son. The Spirit of God is essential to your life and to your relationship with the entire Godhead. He's the illuminator of all spiritual truth and the doorway into the divine. He takes that which is unknown to fallen humanity and makes it a clear and unmistakable reality in our lives.

THE SPIRIT IS SPEAKING...

When you consider your life, do you need somebody to turn the light on? That's the role of the Holy Spirit.

Do you need some wind in your sails? Invite the Spirit to breathe new life into your soul.

Do you want a deeper and more meaningful relationship with almighty God? Then you must understand the Holy Spirit's role in your life. Once you come to know the Spirit in all His fullness, you'll see heaven opened up before you.

Consider what you *do* know about God. Oh, there's much more to learn, but take a moment and thank God for revealing Himself to you. The fact that you're reading this book is an indication that God wants you to experience a deeper relationship with Him. So ask the Holy Spirit to help you see God more clearly. Ask Him to communicate the deep things of God to your spirit.

Finally, commit your life to respond to everything He says. A heart of ready obedience frees the Holy Spirit to speak into your life, because He knows you'll respond when He speaks.

CHAPTER 2

THE EVER-PRESENT GOD

My Father has been working until now, and I have been
working.... Most assuredly, I say to you, the Son can do
nothing of Himself, but what He sees the Father do; for
whatever He does, the Son also does in like manner. For
the Father loves the Son, and shows Him all things that
He Himself does; and He will show Him greater works
than these, that you may marvel.

—JOHN 5:17, 19–20

T he word *God* in today's culture is no longer understood as it was in times past. The secular culture has misused God's name and stripped it of its original meaning. There was a day when the idea of God as the creator and sustainer of the universe was presupposed and accepted as truth. In fact, the Bible doesn't even attempt to prove God's existence, for it didn't have to. Instead, the Bible readily accepts His existence as an undeniable fact, with the assumption that everyone believes in God in some form or another.

Plural form of El.

Our English word *God* translates the Hebrew words *El* and *Elohim,* which were essentially generic terms meaning "god" or "mighty one." They convey a transcendent being upon whom everything in the universe depends. Yet God is much more than a transcendent being who dwells somewhere in the sky. He's a personal God who's very active in the world in which we live.

GOD IS AT WORK

When Jesus said, "My Father has been working until now" (John 5:17), He was pointing to a simple yet profound truth: the heavenly Father is working all around us, and He has been from the beginning of time.

Whether you see Him at work is irrelevant to the fact of God's presence in our world. He is actively and intimately involved in both the affairs of this world and the details of your life.

So the role of the Holy Spirit is not to bring God's presence to the world, but to reveal it. His presence must be revealed because, as we've previously mentioned, sin causes spiritual deadness that blinds our hearts to God's activity; we cannot see Him or respond to His activity unaided by His Spirit.

When Jesus talked in John 5 about the Father's work on earth, He went on to say, "The Son can do nothing of Himself, but what He sees the Father do; for whatever He does, the Son also does in like manner. For the Father loves the Son, and shows Him all things that He Himself does" (verses 19–20). All that Jesus did on earth was in response to what He saw the Father doing. The intriguing implication is that the Father had to show Jesus what He was doing. Even the Son of God had to have His eyes opened to the activity of His Father.

The most important element in what Jesus is saying here is that little word *loves:* "The Father loves the Son, and shows Him all things." The same is true with us. Our heavenly Father desires a love relationship with us that's real and practical. So He gives us the Holy Spirit to help us know and respond to His purposes in our lives.

Jesus likened our love relationship with God to that between a father and child, and He taught us about the Holy Spirit's connection to it: "If you then, being evil, know how to give good gifts to your children, how much more will your heavenly Father give the Holy Spirit to those who ask Him!" (Luke 11:13).

"YOU ARE NOT ALONE"

I (Mel) will never forget a lady in our community who walked into our church looking very uncomfortable. Her story was of a fascinating journey of someone seeking truth in all the wrong places.

A student of languages, she had traveled to Europe in her younger years, where she met some Islamic men in Paris. Intrigued by their belief system, she moved to Syria to learn Arabic and study the Koran. Eventually she married a Muslim and practiced that religious system for twenty years.

In her attempt to please God, she spent many an hour with the prayer mat out, making sure she was facing the right direction and reciting the correct prayers in just the right order. She also fasted the prescribed number of days.

But when health issues threatened her family, she found herself at rock bottom. In her painful difficulties, she came to the realization that "religious activity" and a "relationship with God" were by no means the same thing. She tossed away the prayer mat, got down on her knees, and prayed as she'd never prayed before—from the bottom of her heart. She cried out to her parents, who had passed away, but there was nothing. She cried out to Allah, but still the pain remained.

Suddenly she recalled a picture of Jesus she had seen at church in her childhood. The image was as real and vivid as the day she first saw it. So she cried out to Jesus—and got an answer. The answer was, "You are not alone." It was as if a warm blanket had been wrapped around her, and she felt complete peace. She realized that God was with her.

Though her encounter with God was real, she didn't know what to do about it. So she came to our church and made an appointment to meet with me. As I shared the gospel with her, she wept. She exclaimed, "How could I have wasted so much time and energy for so long? I've spent years searching for truth, but my search led me further and further away. Even as a child being dragged to church, I just never got the Father, Son, and Holy Spirit thing—I just couldn't fathom it." Now, in an instant, the truth was clear to her: "God has been everywhere—all around me—the whole time! All I had to do was be still, open my heart, and surrender to Him."

Her life is now totally changed. She described her encounter with God as being like hot water poured over a tea bag. Once the water hit, it permeated her life and released a fragrance she'd never before experienced. It was as if she were alive for the first time. The blinders were off, and she could finally see life as it was meant to be. The Spirit of God had taken away her spiritual blindness and given her sight.

"I look back on my life," she said, "and along the way there were many obvious signs of God working in my life. But I just couldn't see them." Now that she's born again of the Spirit, she has light to see God and respond in faith to His work in her life and to the love relationship He has initiated.

SEEING SPIRITUAL ACTIVITY

The Bible has many stories of people being made aware of God's activity. One of our favorites is that of the prophet Elisha and his servant in 2 Kings 6. Elisha was being hunted by the king of Syria, who was at war with Israel. The Syrian king was determined to do away with Elisha, because he had a special God-given ability to forewarn the Israelites about the Syrians' every move.

Sent by the king, a Syrian force came by cover of darkness and surrounded the city where Elisha and his servant were spending the night. The two men had no hope of escape.

Early in the morning, as Elisha's servant got up to make breakfast, he realized they were surrounded by "horses and chariots and a great army" (6:14). An entire army had been sent after one man! Terrified, the servant cried out, "Alas, my master! What shall we do?" (6:15)

But Elisha saw something much different than what the servant saw. The prophet's response to their situation was not fear, but confidence in God. He told his servant, "Do not fear, for those who are with us are more than those who are with them" (6:16).

You can imagine what the servant must have thought: "The old guy has lost it! There are only two of us against a mighty army. We don't stand a chance!" He might have turned to the prophet and asked, "Are you seeing what I'm seeing?" And that was the critical question, for they were *not* perceiving the same thing. The servant had the ability to see only his physical surroundings. But Elisha was enabled by the Holy Spirit to see the whole spectrum of reality. The servant saw the activity of men; Elisha saw the activity of God.

Elisha prayed, "LORD…open his eyes that he may see." Immediately the Lord opened the servant's spiritual eyes, and he saw what Elisha saw. "And behold, the mountain was full of horses and chariots of fire all around Elisha" (6:17).

What a difference it makes when you see God's activity! Fear turns to courage. The Spirit of God turns a hopeless situation into an assured, overwhelming victory. It's all dependent on the difference between seeing the circumstances from a human point of view or from God's eternal perspective.

What was true for Elisha is also true for us today: God is actively at work all around us—and if we learn to walk with Him and are willing to adjust our lives to His activity, we'll recognize His activity and live with confidence and hope.

What would you see if God "pulled back the curtain" and let you know what He's doing?

One thing you would see is a raging spiritual battle. As Paul said,

We are not fighting against people made of flesh and blood, but against the evil rulers and authorities of the unseen world, against those mighty powers of darkness who rule this world, and against wicked spirits in the heavenly realms. (Ephesians 6:12, NLT)

Only God can bring the victory in this spiritual battle. The key to that victory is not what we're doing for God, but what *He* is doing around us. Once we learn to recognize Him, we can join Him in His great plan of salvation.

ENCOUNTERS WITH GOD

The foundation of our faith is not doctrine, but an encounter with God. Doctrines are simply the attempt to help us understand the God we've already encountered. In the Old Testament, encounters with God allowed people to know Him. Once they saw Him work, they understood more of who He is, and they could respond to Him in faith.

These moments of encounter often resulted in the people giving Him another name. In fact, all the names of God in the Bible are simply a testimony of God's presence in people's lives. Knowing and understanding these specific names for Him will help us know how He wants to act in our lives today. God is not a transcendent being who's unknowable; He encounters our very lives, meeting us in the real world.

King David was one who knew the Lord well. He had many encounters and experiences with the Lord, and he took many of these real-life situations to the Lord in prayer. In those moments he found that God was everything he needed.

Consider David's words in Psalm 23 as an outline of some of the biblical names of God that correspond to how He works in our lives:

The LORD is my shepherd…	*Jehovah Rohi* "The Lord our shepherd"
I shall not want…	*Jehovah Jireh* "The Lord who provides"
He makes me to lie down in green pastures; He leads me beside the still waters…	*Jehovah Shalom* "The Lord our peace"
He restores my soul…	*Jehovah Rophi* "The Lord who heals"
He leads me in the paths of righteousness for His name's sake…	*Jehovah Tsidkenu* "The Lord our righteousness"
Yea though I walk through the valley of the shadow of death, I will fear no evil, for You are with me. Your rod and Your staff, they comfort me…	*Jehovah Shammah* "The Lord is there"
You prepare a table before me in the presence of my enemies…	*Jehovah Nissi* "The Lord our banner"
You anoint my head with oil; my cup runs over…	*Jehovah Mekoddishkem* "The Lord who sanctifies"

Surely goodness and mercy shall follow me all the days of my life; and I will dwell in the house of the LORD forever.

For generations, Psalm 23 has comforted people all over the world as they see how God cares for His people. This care is reflected in His names, which represent how He encountered His people in times past. His names reveal His character and help us comprehend what kind of relationship we can expect from Him. He's a personal God, a covenant God, a God who desires a relationship with His people—a relationship that makes a difference in our daily lives.

When we speak of encounters with God, we're at the same time talking about revelation by the Spirit of God. The Spirit is God's agent on earth to communicate truth to the spirit within human beings. He opens His people's eyes, gives us wisdom, empowers us for service, and stirs us into action. Just because God is active and working doesn't mean people understand or will respond in faith. The Holy Spirit must give us the ability to both recognize and respond to God.

THE SIGN OF HIS PRESENCE

In the Old Testament, when God chose to do His work through people, He sent His Spirit upon them. His presence in their lives enabled them to do His will and gave them confidence that He was with them in times of trouble.

Consider some of the many people who experienced God's Spirit as a part of their divine call to service:

Then I will come down and talk with you [*Moses*] there. I
will take of the *Spirit* that is upon you and will put the same
upon them. (Numbers 11:17)

The LORD said to Moses: "Take *Joshua* the son of Nun with
you, a man in whom is the *Spirit.* (Numbers 27:18)

The *Spirit of the LORD* came upon him [*Othniel*], and he
judged Israel. (Judges 3:10)

But the *Spirit of the LORD* came upon *Gideon.* (Judges 6:34)

Then the *Spirit of the LORD* came upon *Jephthah.* (Judges
11:29)

And the *Spirit of the LORD* came mightily upon him [*Sam-son*]. (Judges 14:6)

Then the *Spirit of the LORD* will come upon you [*Saul*], and
you will prophesy with them and be turned into another man.
And let it be, when these signs come to you, that you do as
the occasion demands; for *God is with you.* (1 Samuel 10:6–7)

And the *Spirit of the LORD* came upon *David* from that day
forward. (1 Samuel 16:13)

Now the *Spirit of God* came upon *Azariah* the son of Oded.
(2 Chronicles 15:1)

Then the *Spirit of God* came upon *Zechariah* the son of
Jehoiada the priest. (2 Chronicles 24:20)

"Son of man, stand on your feet, and I will speak to you."
Then the *Spirit* entered me [*Ezekiel*] when He spoke to me.
(Ezekiel 2:1–2)

But truly I [*Micah*] am full of power by the *Spirit of the
LORD*. (Micah 3:8)

Over and over, God sent His Spirit upon people to enable them
to fulfill His purposes. But it was more than just equipping them for
service. The sending of the Spirit was at the same time a sign that
His presence was there. When the Spirit of God was present, God
was in their midst. And the Spirit enabled His chosen servants to
recognize His activity and make the adjustments to obey the will of
God.

ONE FOR ALL

Even as God was making His presence known through prophets,
judges, and kings who were filled with the Holy Spirit, He was always

looking forward to the day when His Spirit would be poured out on *all* people. This promise was given through the prophet Joel:

> And it shall come to pass afterward
> That I will pour out My Spirit on all flesh;
> Your sons and your daughters shall
>   prophesy,
> Your old men shall dream dreams,
> Your young men shall see visions.
> And also on My menservants and on My
>   maidservants
> I will pour out My Spirit in those days....
> And it shall come to pass
> That whoever calls on the name of the
>   LORD
> Shall be saved. (Joel 2:28–29, 32)

A relationship with God is not just for prophets, judges, and kings; it's for all His people. It's for sons and daughters. It's for the old and the young. It's for the wealthy and the poor, the powerful and the weak. When all of these have the spiritual capacity to see the activity of God in their lives, they also have the ability to call upon His name and receive His saving deliverance and power.

The gift of the Spirit at Pentecost was recognized and foretold by others in addition to the prophet Joel. Ezekiel prophesied of a day when the Spirit of God would be freely poured out on the people of God: "'I will not hide My face from them anymore; for *I shall have poured out My Spirit* on the house of Israel,' says the Lord GOD" (39:29). Isaiah talked about the judgment of God "until the Spirit is poured upon us from on high" (32:15).

Later Isaiah wrote:

> Thus says the LORD who made you
> And formed you from the womb, who
>   will help you:
> "Fear not, O Jacob My servant;
> And you, Jeshurun, whom I have chosen.
> For I will pour water on him who is thirsty,
> And floods on the dry ground;
> *I will pour My Spirit on your descendants,*
> And My blessing on your offspring."
>   (44:2–3)

The Lord also spoke through Zechariah to say, "I will pour on the house of David and on the inhabitants of Jerusalem *the Spirit of grace and supplication*" (12:10).

Although the Day of Pentecost was planned in the heart of God from the very beginning, it would not take place until the Son of God had come; it *couldn't* happen until Jesus fulfilled His role in God's great plan of salvation. Until the fallen and sin-filled world was dealt with through the death and resurrection of the Savior, the Holy Spirit had to wait. For Jesus is "the way, the truth, and the life" (John 14:6)—giving all people access to a love relationship with the heavenly Father. Christ's work had to be complete before the outpouring of the Spirit could fall upon the human race.

THE SPIRIT IS SPEAKING...

Throughout the Bible, God did His work on earth through the Holy Spirit. People throughout history have experienced the powerful work of the Spirit in their lives, and they've been used of God to impact the world in which they lived. But this is not a history lesson. This is *your* opportunity to experience the mighty work of the Spirit *today.* Your world desperately needs godly men and women who will yield themselves to the Spirit and allow God to touch the world through them.

The Day of Pentecost was more than a historical event; it was God's announcement to the world that a new day had arrived. The Spirit was poured out upon all who would believe in Jesus from that day forward.

So what about you? Has the Spirit been poured out in your life? What is the evidence that the Spirit of God has taken up residence in your life?

Take a moment and talk with God about His presence in your life. Do you really want to experience Him in His fullness? Or would you rather lay low and not get involved? Are you one who wants to see the mighty power of God, or do you want to just slip into heaven doing the bare minimum? What do you think God wants for your life? Put aside your desires, and ask God to show you His purposes for your life.

PART TWO

Gift of the Spirit in the Life of the Lord Jesus

CHAPTER 3

GIFTED TO SERVE

*When all the people were baptized, it came to pass that
Jesus also was baptized; and while He prayed, the
heaven was opened. And the Holy Spirit descended in
bodily form like a dove upon Him.*

—LUKE 3:21–22

The nature of Jesus as the divine Son of God is an inspiration to all who put their faith in Him. Yet there are some who set aside His example as unattainable. After all, Jesus is God and we're not.

But before you dismiss the example of Jesus as something you can never experience, examine more closely the life He led. It's true He came to earth as our Savior, but He also came as our example.

As He served the heavenly Father, He needed *help*. That's right. He had to be "gifted" to serve. And that same divine enabling is available to you.

HUMBLE BEGINNINGS

Have you noticed that the gospel writers never mention any of Jesus' physical attributes? Nor do they speak at all about His human talents or abilities. Instead they write about the wisdom and power displayed through His life. They talk about the work of the Holy Spirit in Him as He fulfilled the Father's purpose.

The key to understanding the life of Christ is to recognize the work of the Holy Spirit in that life. Once you see the relationship between Jesus and the Holy Spirit, you'll understand how the Spirit will also work in your life. For the Spirit who gifted Jesus to serve His heavenly Father is the same one who will also gift you for service.

Jesus humbled Himself when He was made a man. It's hard for us to fully comprehend the distance from the throne room of heaven to the stable in Bethlehem. It's even harder for us to know what it means for the God of the universe to be confined to the limited and fragile body of a human being. The incarnation was an extreme example of God's love, that Jesus would take upon Himself the humble state of man. In that startling event, eternity intersected with time, the heavens with the earth, and God with man.

This moment was described a thousand years earlier by David in Psalm 8:4–5: "What is man that You are mindful of him, and the son of man that You visit him? For you have made him a little lower than the angels." The King of kings took a place lower than the servants in heaven's throne room. More than that, He came to earth not as a ruler of the people, but as a common person, the son of a carpenter.

The writer of Hebrews reflected with awe on the humble estate of this one "who was made a little lower than the angels, for the suffering of death…that He, by the grace of God, might taste death for everyone." We read further how God, in order to bring "many sons to glory," saw fit "to make the captain of their salvation perfect through sufferings. For both He who sanctifies and those who are being sanctified are all of one, for which reason He is not ashamed to call them brethren" (2:9–11).

The coming of Christ was nothing less than amazing, and the circumstances surrounding His birth fully reflected the wonder of it all. The scene was something only God could have planned. We read that angels—heavenly beings, superior to us in wisdom and power—came to converse with lowly shepherds. Angels came from the throne room of a holy God to a field full of sheep. Angels, who look upon God's splendor and glory, came to a world of sin and darkness. Angels, who serve God, announced to the shepherds that *God is coming to serve them* by meeting mankind's greatest need.

Have you ever wondered what was going on in the minds of the angels that very first Christmas? They came to make an announcement they could hardly believe. As servants of God, they aren't omniscient like God; they don't know all things. But they must have known prophecies of old, and they understood what was about to happen. I can't help but think it was a glorious moment. The God whom they served in the heavenlies was coming to earth in the form of a baby! Could it be true? Imagine how absurd that might seem to an angel who understands exactly how powerful God is—and how weak a human being is.

But that's the genius of God. He knew that the humble condition of Jesus would be our hope. The world would finally see what it looks like for a man to walk with God. They would see the life *we* were meant to live.

THE EXAMPLE OF JESUS

Jesus is the example, the model, of how we can live in relation to God. Although He was God, He chose to set aside what was rightfully His and take on the frail and limited abilities of the human race. When the apostle Paul presented the humble attitude of Jesus as our example to follow, he emphasized the human condition He assumed:

> Let this mind be in you which was also in Christ Jesus, who, being in the form of God, did not consider it robbery to be equal with God, but made Himself of no reputation, taking the form of a bondservant, and coming in the likeness of men. And being found in appearance as a man, He humbled Himself and became obedient to the point of death, even the death of the cross. (Philippians 2:5–8)

When Jesus took on human flesh, He chose to live under the limitations that come with a physical body. That doesn't mean He ceased to be divine, but He willingly set aside His rights as God and lived as a human. And being limited by His physical condition, He was forced to rely upon the Holy Spirit as His source of wisdom and power.

We see the presence of the Holy Spirit in Jesus' life in a clear and visible way at the time of His baptism. Something spectacular happened there at the Jordan River, something that initiated a new role for the Spirit in His life:

> When all the people were baptized, it came to pass that Jesus also was baptized; and while He prayed, the heaven was opened. And the Holy Spirit descended in bodily form like a dove upon Him, and a voice came from heaven which said, "You are My beloved Son; in You I am well pleased." (Luke 3:21–22)

This moment represented the beginning of a new stage in Jesus' life, a special anointing by the Father for extraordinary and demanding tasks.

From the moment Jesus began His public ministry, the work of the Holy Spirit enabled Him to do everything the Father asked of Him. The Scriptures make this clear. Immediately after Jesus' baptism, Luke tells us, "Jesus, *being filled with the Holy Spirit,* returned from the Jordan and was led by the Spirit into the wilderness" (4:1). Immediately after being tempted in the wilderness by the devil, "Jesus returned in the *power of the Spirit* to Galilee, and news of Him went out through all the surrounding region" (4:14).

Jesus then went to Nazareth, where we see Him speak with clarity of the assignment God had given Him. Standing in the synagogue, He turned in the Scriptures to Isaiah and read:

> *The Spirit of the LORD is upon Me,*
> Because He has anointed Me
> To preach the gospel to the poor;
> He has sent Me to heal the brokenhearted,
> To proclaim liberty to the captives
> And recovery of sight to the blind,
> To set at liberty those who are oppressed;
> To proclaim the acceptable year of the
>   LORD....
> Today this Scripture is fulfilled in your
>   hearing. (4:18–19, 21)

So we see the pattern: the assignment was given by the Father, accepted by the Son, and fulfilled through the working power of the Spirit.

That pattern is exactly what will happen in our lives as children of God.

EQUIPPED FOR THE ASSIGNMENT

Jesus fulfilled His assignment as a man filled with the Holy Spirit. He was a man in every sense of the word, but He lived beyond His human ability because He yielded His life to the work of the Holy Spirit. As a result, He was able to fulfill everything the Father wanted Him to accomplish. "My food is to do the will of Him who sent Me," He told His disciples, "and to finish His work" (John 4:34).

Jesus suggested the limitations of His ability when He said, "The Son can do nothing of Himself, but what He sees the Father do" (John 5:19). To those who questioned where He received His wisdom, He answered, "My doctrine is not Mine, but His who sent Me. If anyone wills to do His will, he shall know concerning the doctrine, whether it is from God or whether I speak on My own authority" (John 7:16–17). He said to others, "I do nothing of Myself; but as My Father taught Me, I speak these things. And He who sent Me is with Me. The Father has not left Me alone, for I always do those things that please Him" (John 8:28–29). Likewise Jesus told His disciples in the upper room, "The words that I speak to you I do not speak on My own authority; but the Father who dwells in Me does the works" (John 14:10).

Never overlook the source of Jesus' power while He walked on earth in the flesh. We tend to excuse His miracles by saying, "It was easy for Him; He was God!" But when the Son of God chose to come and dwell among us, He laid aside what was rightfully His and lived like a man. "Although He existed in the form of God, [Jesus] did not regard equality with God a thing to be grasped, but emptied Himself, taking the form of a bond-servant, and being made in the likeness of men" (Philippians 2:6–7, NASB).

Jesus chose to live with all the limitations of a human being. Why? Because He couldn't take our place unless He first took up our condition. Salvation was dependent upon a *man* named Jesus dying on the cross for our sins. His life is therefore a demonstration of the way in which *we* can live, full of the Holy Spirit.

Even the teaching Jesus gave the disciples after He'd risen from the dead was accomplished through the Spirit. Luke told us that Jesus ascended into heaven "after He *through the Holy Spirit* had given commandments to the apostles whom He had chosen" (Acts 1:2). From beginning to end, the Holy Spirit was at work in the life of Jesus.

While on earth, we human beings are always in need of the Holy Spirit in our lives. That was true of Jesus, and it's true of us. That's why the final commandment of Jesus to the disciples was to wait for the coming of the Holy Spirit upon their lives. He knew they couldn't do the Father's will without the Spirit; but *in* the Spirit all things were possible.

And so it happened. Once the Spirit came upon the apostles, they began doing everything the people had seen Jesus do. They healed the sick, raised the dead, and taught with great authority and power—and lives were changed.

It can happen that way in our lives and ministry as well. For the Holy Spirit who came upon Jesus is exactly the same Holy Spirit given to you and me.

JESUS KNOWS

To know the life of Jesus is a great encouragement to us today. For no matter what challenges we face, He understands. He too has lived in this fallen and sinful world. He has endured much suffering in His body, just like the rest of us.

I (Henry) will never forget walking into the brokenness of a poor Indian reservation in northern Canada. Our church had felt the call of God to bring light into a dark world, and the reservations were extremely dark and full of pain.

An older lady there said, "I've watched so many of my children and family die." And it was true; the mortality rate on the reservation was very high. Alcoholism was rampant, leading to various tragedies from traffic accidents to suicides, stabbings, and other acts of violence.

But then this lady met Jesus and was gloriously saved. Her life was radically changed. Her sorrow turned to joy. She said, "The pain has been unbearable, even to the point where I didn't know if I could go on. But now I'm full of joy, for I know Jesus Christ as my Lord and Savior. And He reminded me that He knew much pain, He endured much sorrow, and He understood what was in my heart."

We serve a God who knows our pain. He understands exactly what this world brings to our lives. Read slowly and reflectively these words spoken about our Lord by the prophet Isaiah:

> He is despised and rejected by men,
> A Man of sorrows and acquainted with
>   grief.
> And we hid, as it were, our faces from
>   Him;
> He was despised, and we did not esteem
>   Him.
> Surely He has borne our griefs
> And carried our sorrows;
> Yet we esteemed Him stricken,
> Smitten by God, and afflicted.
> But He was wounded for our
>   transgressions,
> He was bruised for our iniquities;
> The chastisement for our peace was upon
>   Him,
> And by His stripes we are healed.
> All we like sheep have gone astray;
> We have turned, every one, to his own
>   way;

And the LORD has laid on Him the
    iniquity of us all.
He was oppressed and He was afflicted,
Yet He opened not His mouth;
He was led as a lamb to the slaughter,
And as a sheep before its shearers is silent,
So He opened not His mouth. (53:3–7)

Yes, Jesus lived as a man who understands the harsh reality of sin and its consequences. Yet He did it with such grace. He lived with such confidence and purpose. He lived His life victoriously because of His love relationship with the Father and through the power of the Holy Spirit. And when life is caving in all around you, His presence in your life makes all the difference. He has been there; He knows what you're feeling.

But there's much more than just endurance; there's hope. The Native American woman had found comfort for her pain, but she also found purpose for living. She said, "I'm so full of joy because I've met Jesus, and I know He's going to help me reach the rest of my family. I don't need to see any more deaths. Christ will give the victory!"

What happened? How is it that a poor and broken grandmother, forgotten and abandoned in a faraway place, could find true joy? How is it that the lowest on the socioeconomic scale can relate to the King of kings and Lord of lords? Simply this: she found a con-nection to Him who knew much sorrow, but overcame. And the Holy Spirit who filled His life was now in her life. Jesus took her hand in His and walked her through a difficult time.

Jesus learned how to bring glory to God in a physical body, even in the context of a fallen and sinful world. He found strength as He drew close to the Father and walked in the power of the Spirit. The filling of the Spirit allowed Him to endure, overcome, and conquer this world.

And the same gift He received from the Father is now the gift He gives to all who put their trust in Him.

THE SPIRIT IS SPEAKING...

You may be one who wants to live in victory and make a difference in the world, but the world is winning. Perhaps you're not experi-encing the Bible's promise to be an overcomer; instead, the world has overcome you. And the life of Jesus seems so foreign.

Let me assure you, Jesus knows what you're going through. He knows your weaknesses. He knows your struggles.

> For we do not have a High Priest who cannot sympathize
> with our weaknesses, but was in all points tempted as we are,
> yet without sin. Let us therefore come boldly to the throne

of grace, that we may obtain mercy and find grace to help in time of need. (Hebrews 4:15–16)

So come to Jesus, that He might show you the way to abundant life. He'll help you know the way *He lived*—full of the Holy Spirit.

You've worked hard and tried your best. But you have yet to experience what you know is available to you in Christ. Do you want to know Jesus' secret? It was the work of the Holy Spirit in His life.

Have you been living according to your natural abilities without considering what the Holy Spirit desires to do in your life? Have your abilities even kept you from seeking Him with all your heart? Come to Jesus and learn from Him. He'll show you the way.

You may want to pause in this moment and pray in response to what you've heard Him speak to you in this chapter.

Chapter 4

HIS GIFT TO GIVE

*Behold, I send the Promise of My Father upon you; but
tarry in the city of Jerusalem until you are endued with
power from on high.*

—Luke 24:49

God has kingdom work to do on earth, and He is looking for
believers through whom He can do His work. We're looking
for better methods; God is looking for better men and women.

When it comes to serving God, total dependence is better than
talent and determination. Our best efforts will always come short of
what God could do through our lives if only we would learn to trust
Him.

When we talk about God's work in His people, we're talking
about the Holy Spirit. For the Holy Spirit to work in our lives, the
critically necessary element is our relationship to Jesus Christ—because Christ is the one who sends the gift of the Holy Spirit to shape
and mold us into His image.

JESUS EXPLAINS

You'll notice that Jesus didn't take much time to explain the Holy Spirit early in His ministry. He was busy just doing the assignment the Father had for Him. But there came a time when He needed to teach the disciples about the Spirit. He knew they would need the Spirit's equipping for *their* assignment from the Father. The disciples had seen many miracles through His life, and they needed to understand that the same power demonstrated in His life would soon be available to them.

The mystery of Pentecost is that the living, reigning Lord of the universe would now come to dwell in the life of every believer. How does one explain that? In reality, no one can fully understand it; it's something you just have to experience. And yet you can prepare and ready yourself to receive that gift. So in John 14–16, Jesus began making incredible statements about the enabling that heaven would bring to the disciples. He was preparing His followers for Pentecost, which was God's provision for them to fulfill their assignment.

Jesus said to the disciples, "I will pray the Father, and He will give you another Helper, that He may abide with you forever" (John 14:16). That phrase *another Helper* doesn't mean another of a different kind, but another of the same kind. The Helper will be just like Christ. According to the Scripture, the Father, Son, and Holy Spirit are distinct in person but always function together: one God in three persons. When you encounter one, you encounter all.

One of the characteristics of the Holy Spirit is that He always exalts Christ. So as you experience the Holy Spirit, you'll at the same time experience the Spirit of Christ. That's why Jesus could say to the disciples, "It is to your advantage that I go away; for if I do not go away, the Helper will not come to you" (John 16:7). For if the disciples had the Holy Spirit within them, they would have all there is of Jesus as well.

While in the days of His flesh, Jesus could only be in one place at a time. But after the Spirit came at Pentecost, He could be in every believer around the world at the same time. That was a totally different experience from what the disciples had previously known.

When Jesus spoke to the disciples in the upper room that night, He knew He would soon be arrested, beaten, crucified, and buried. He also knew He would then be resurrected and ascend back to heaven to reign at the right hand of the Father. That's why this teaching on the Holy Spirit was crucial for the disciples to understand. So listen to what Jesus said about the Helper:

> The Spirit of truth, whom the world cannot receive, because it neither sees Him nor knows Him; but you know Him, for He dwells with you and will be in you. I will not leave you orphans; I will come to you. (John 14:17–18)

Though the disciples didn't fully understand what Jesus was saying at this time, He was foretelling what was about to happen: *the*

Holy Spirit who dwells "with you" will soon be "in you." A dramatic change was about to happen in their relationship to the Lord. They'd experienced the Holy Spirit "with them" through the life of Jesus. They'd seen the Spirit's power in the miracles of Jesus and His wisdom in the teaching of Jesus and His fruit in the character of Jesus. The disciples had even known the privilege of experiencing the Spirit's borrowed power, as it were, when Jesus empowered them to go out and minister in His name (Luke 10:1–20). They had known many wonderful times *with* the Holy Spirit—but nothing would compare with the gift of Pentecost when the Holy Spirit would dwell *in* them.

When Jesus said, "I will not leave you...I will come to you," He was talking about the gift of Pentecost. He would come to the disciples through the gift of the Holy Spirit. To be filled with the Spirit is to be filled with Christ.

Don't let anybody tell you that once Christ ascended to the Father and sent the Holy Spirit, we no longer relate to Christ but to the Spirit. That's just not true. The Spirit brings *Christ* to be real and personal in our lives. Paul said that the eternal purpose of God is "*Christ in you,* the hope of glory" (Colossians 1:27). He went on to say that "*in Him* [Christ] dwells all the fullness of the Godhead bodily; and you are complete in Him, who is the head of all principality and power" (Colossians 2:9–10).

Christ is our life. But we experience our relationship with Him through the presence of the Holy Spirit. With Paul's statements in mind, let's go back to John 14 and review how Jesus described His new relationship with the disciples:

> A little while longer and the world will see Me no more, but you will see Me. Because I live, you will live also. At that day you will know that I am in My Father, and you in Me, and I in you. (John 14:19–20)

What was Jesus talking about? He was talking about Pentecost. That radical moment purposed by God was about to take place. Pentecost was the event that would take everything Christ accomplished while on earth and apply it to the life of every believer for all time. His relationship with the twelve disciples would be multiplied many times over through the presence of the Spirit. In essence, Jesus was saying to the disciples, "I need to go back to the Father and reign from on high. So I'll send My Spirit to dwell within you, so He can implement My will concerning your life."

Jesus is the one who gives the gift of the Spirit because He's also the one designated to be Lord of our lives; it's *Jesus* we're to obey. Our relationship with Jesus is the key to experiencing the powerful work of the Holy Spirit. If we're not walking in a love relationship with Jesus and obeying His will for our lives, there's no need for the Holy Spirit to enable our lives. We don't need the Holy Spirit's power if we're in rebellion against Jesus Christ. Pentecost was heaven's gift to enable those who would obey the Lord.

OBEDIENCE CHANGES THE RELATIONSHIP

Peter was a man who attended our church for several years. He was a good man, faithful to attend worship and pleasant to be around. But he was careful to keep his distance and not get too involved. He'd been a Christian most of his life, but his unwillingness to serve the Lord created a distance from the Lord. Peter's countenance often seemed heavy, for he knew he was going through the motions without having a real relationship with Christ. His spirit was troubled, for he had the shell of Christianity without the substance to sustain it. Over time, he began to look more like the world than a child of God.

Then I (Mel) started to hear his name mentioned around the church. I saw his name among those of the mission team going to do disaster relief. He began showing up at an early morning men's prayer meeting. I saw him cooking hamburgers at the church fellowship. I heard of a Bible study he was leading downtown at his place of work.

But the greatest change was the look in his eyes. His countenance had changed; he was full of joy. In times past when I would approach him, he would look away awkwardly and not have much to say. Now his smile was captivating as he talked with excitement about the things of the Lord.

One day I stopped him in the hallway and asked him, "What happened to you?" He laughed and said, "Isn't it great! Once I decided to trust the Lord and obey, He decided He could trust me with the power to do the work. I can't believe what I was missing. Once I decided to obey Him, I came to know His presence like never before."

The Holy Spirit doesn't need to equip you for what you're *not* going to do, so if you're in rebellion against Jesus and refusing His right to be Lord, He doesn't need to send the Holy Spirit to equip you for service. And, tragically, you miss out on the joy that He brings.

So let the Holy Spirit deal with anything that's keeping you from obeying Christ.

JESUS WILL IMMERSE YOU

A passage in Luke 3 connects the ministry of Jesus and the Holy Spirit in dramatic fashion. John the Baptist is on the scene, preparing the way for the coming of Christ. In the process, people ask John if he's the Messiah, for they see something about his life that suggests he's more than just another prophet.

John, however, explains the difference between himself and the coming Messiah, and it's almost alarming. John baptizes with water, but he says that the Messiah will baptize with "the Holy Spirit and fire" (Luke 3:16).

At this point, we need to clarify what the word *baptism* means. Don't think of a religious ceremony or church practice. The Greek word literally means "to immerse, plunge, or submerge." When Jesus comes, He'll immerse you in the Holy Spirit and in fire. You'll know you've met the Christ, for your whole life will be completely encompassed by the Spirit and fire.

The Holy Spirit isn't simply a gift Jesus gives us, but a Person who captures us, purges us, and directs our lives. When this happens, it's a moment that cannot be mistaken. All who have encountered Jesus will at the same time experience the coming of the Holy Spirit and fire upon their lives.

Could that be said of your life? Can you identify your encounter with Christ and the work of the Spirit upon your life? According to John the Baptist, being immersed in the Spirit and fire is evidence that you've met the Christ. He said that a "winnowing fork" is in Christ's hand, that He might "thoroughly clear His threshing floor." Our lives will be thrown up by the fork and the wheat separated from the chaff. The wheat will be gathered, and the chaff will burn "with unquenchable fire" (Matthew 3:12, NASB).

If you cannot identify the separating process of the Holy Spirit in your life, could it be you haven't truly met the Christ? For Christ brings with Him the person of the Holy Spirit. And if the Holy Spirit isn't at work in your life, you're just practicing cultural Christian religion rather than experiencing the living Christ. To meet Christ is to endure the winnowing fork and its active work, whereby all that is unacceptable is identified and removed from your life.

The chaff represents the impurities in our lives. Malachi 3:2–3 likens the coming of the Lord to a refiner's fire or launderers' soap. When fine metals like silver or gold are put into the heat, the dross is separated and rises to the top. All the impurities are then skimmed off to leave pure silver or pure gold.

Fire purifies; it has the power to remove impurity. Have you noticed that the presence of Christ includes the purifying presence of the Holy Spirit to bring to the surface the impurities in your life? Has the *Holy* Spirit revealed *unholy* living in you? You cannot receive Christ into your life without being immersed in the Holy Spirit. Jesus brings the Holy Spirit with Him!

Consider the statement Jesus made in John 14:9. Philip had asked Jesus to show the Father to the disciples. Jesus answered, "Have I been with you so long, and yet you have not known Me, Philip? He who has seen Me has seen the Father." To look at Jesus was to see the Father, for He was the true image of the Father's love, His kindness, His power, and all that God is.

With that image in mind, consider the work of the Holy Spirit in your life. Jesus immerses your life in the Holy Spirit and fire to remove all the impurities—so that when people see you, they have an accurate picture of Him. Jesus wants people to see His image when they look at your life.

What an eternal tragedy it would be for a person to look at your life and be turned away from Christ!

There's never an excuse for sin once you've been immersed in the Holy Spirit and fire. You cannot argue, "I've always had a problem with anger, even as a child. People just need to accept me for who I am." That rationale is proof positive that you haven't met Christ, for He brings the winnowing fork. He brings the Holy Spirit and fire to remove anything that doesn't reflect Him.

Before you met Christ, you couldn't help it. Sin had a grip on you. But once you met Christ, He gave you power over sin, and He also desires to burn it away completely. That's why Jesus gives the gift of the Holy Spirit. You won't be able to go with Him until the Spirit does His work to remove your sin.

GOING WITH JESUS

In Acts 1:8, Jesus said, "You shall receive power when the Holy Spirit has come upon you; and you shall be witnesses *to Me.*" We don't go out as witness *for* Him, but *unto* Him. He doesn't send us out on an assignment; we go *with* Him on His assignment. Jesus takes us with Him. So many people have a misguided belief that we're to go *for* Him, but in reality we go *with* Him into this world.

Wherever Jesus takes you, you become the presence of Christ in that place, because His Spirit is in you. As you become witnesses unto Jesus, He's there to enable you to fulfill that assignment.

Now listen to the last two verses found in the gospel of Mark:

So then, after the Lord had spoken to them, He was received up into heaven, and sat down at the right hand of God. And they went out and preached everywhere, the Lord working with them and confirming the word through the accompanying signs. (16:19–20)

NB

Can you see it? The Lord was taken up to the right hand of God, and as the disciples took their assignment of sharing the gospel, He went with them. Through the Holy Spirit, He can be at the right hand of God in heaven and in the life of every believer at the same time.

THE DIVINE IN YOU

The divine nature in you cannot be hidden. It must and it will express itself. A Christian is nothing less than a supernatural being who has had a supernatural experience—and that experience is something more than singing choruses, making a decision, becoming a member of a church, or enjoying Christian gatherings. It is *Christ at the center of your life.*

How does that become real? It becomes reality when you finally grasp that what we call a "presence" is actually a *life.* Paul said, "For to me, to live *is* Christ" (Philippians 1:21); he didn't say, "For me to live is *to be like* Christ" or "*to imitate* Christ."

You cannot imitate Christ, but you *can* allow the Holy Spirit to reveal Christ in you so He's a part of you. Listen again to Paul's words. "It pleased God…to reveal *His Son in me,* that I might preach

He didn't say "imitate me as I imitate Christ."

Him among the Gentiles.... And they glorified *God in me*" (Galatians 1:15–16, 24). Paul knew experientially the presence of the Lord in His life. That can be true of your life as well.

THE SPIRIT IS SPEAKING...

The late Scottish preacher Duncan Campbell wrote insightful words in his book *The Price and Power of Revival*:

> The baptism of the Holy Spirit in its final analysis is not
> manifestations, it is not gifts. The baptism of the Holy Spirit
> in its final analysis is the revelation of Jesus. "God revealed
> His Son in me."

What does this "revealing" look like? What *should* it look like? What could Christ do in us if we would let him?

Are you trying to be like Christ, or are you allowing Christ to be Himself in you? Oh, that we might let Christ be revealed in us! If you desire for Christ to be revealed in your life, you must be immersed in the Holy Spirit.

Take a few moments and consider what you've just read. Did your encounter with Christ also include being immersed in the Spirit? How did you respond?

This relationship we talk about will be unfolded in greater detail throughout this book, but now is a good time to allow the Holy

Spirit to begin His work. For if you want Christ, you must also receive the gift of His Spirit. Then may you say with all humility, "I have been crucified with Christ; it is no longer I who live, but Christ lives in me" (Galatians 2:20).

PART THREE

Power of the Spirit in the Believer's Experience

CHAPTER 5

THE GIFT OF RELATIONSHIP

*And I will pray the Father, and He will give you
another Helper, that He may abide with you forever—
the Spirit of truth, whom the world cannot receive,
because it neither sees Him nor knows Him; but you
know Him, for He dwells with you and will be in you.*

—JOHN 14:16–17

There's often a big difference between the promises of God in Scripture and the daily experience of many Christians. Why is it that countless believers seem to stand powerless before a world desperately needing what we claim to have? Why does the church have so little impact when we're the body of Christ on earth? Why are so many Christians frustrated, sensing that there has to be something more?

There are probably several reasons, but a major one is that Christians are seeking gifts of the Holy Spirit and not the Holy Spirit

Himself. They want power but not a relationship with the One whose presence gives power. They want to do great things for God, but they haven't understood that greatness in the kingdom of God comes out of a relationship with Christ and the filling of the Holy Spirit. They're so enamored with self that they have no idea what's on the heart of God, and they miss out on what He has purposed for their lives.

If we seek the gifts of the Spirit and not the Holy Spirit Himself, we'll always focus on self. We must learn to understand that *there are no gifts apart from an intimate relationship with the Spirit.* And the work of the Spirit is directly connected to the lordship of Christ in our lives.

The greatest single tragedy of the people of God today is that they're missing the fullness of the Spirit. If they only knew what they were missing, they would stop everything and seek Him with all their hearts. For apart from the active presence of the Holy Spirit, there's no possibility of an individual or a church doing anything but practicing religious activity. You may be very active and involved in your church, but without the fullness of the Spirit, you'll miss the power of God. What God is seeking from us is not more activity, but a deeper relationship.

WHAT'S NEW WITH YOU?

For the Christian, faith is not asking for what we don't have, but making use of what God says we already possess. It's simply trusting

God's Word to be true. Nowhere else is this more profoundly true than in what is given us in God's Spirit.

The Bible says every Christian is "a new creation; old things have passed away; behold, all things have become new" (2 Corinthians 5:17). So what's new? Mainly this: you've been forgiven of sin, cleansed of all unrighteousness, clothed in the righteousness of Christ—and given the gift of the Holy Spirit to dwell within you. To be a Christian is to have a new spiritual life, a new relationship with God, a new authority in heaven and on earth, and a new power to serve. All this comes as we receive the gift of the Holy Spirit.

This spiritual transformation deep within a person is at the heart of God's great salvation. Christians are not mere mortals; we're born-again citizens of the kingdom of God who live in a spiritual realm that the unbelieving world cannot understand. So if there's little difference between one who claims to be a Christian and the unbelieving world, something's desperately wrong.

BETTER THAN JESUS AT OUR SIDE

One of the most overlooked verses in the Bible is John 16:7. There Jesus explained, "I tell you the truth. It is to your advantage that I go away; for if I do not go away, the Helper will not come to you; but if I depart, I will send Him to you." What an amazing statement! Jesus told His disciples they would be better off if He left and the

Spirit came. Better to have the Holy Spirit within you than Jesus beside you.

But that's hard to believe. What could possibly be better than having Jesus Christ physically present?

Peter was one who couldn't comprehend what Jesus was saying that night in the upper room. Peter always fought hard to keep Jesus close, even rebuking his Lord when He talked of going to the cross. On the Mount of Transfiguration, it was Peter who wanted to build a permanent structure and stay there. The night before Jesus' crucifixion, it was Peter who boldly proclaimed his allegiance by claiming his willingness to go both to prison and to death with Him. Later, when soldiers went to Gethsemane to arrest Jesus, it was Peter who drew his sword and cut off the ear of a soldier trying to take Him away. Peter was committed to remaining with Jesus at all costs.

It wasn't long, however, before Peter understood what Jesus meant that night. Pentecost came, and the promise of the coming Spirit was fulfilled. Peter and the other disciples were filled with the Holy Spirit, never again to be the same. Peter, who had been self-pleasing, self-trusting, and self-seeking, had now died to self. Peter—full of sin, continually getting into trouble, foolish and impetuous—had now been filled with the Spirit. And the mighty power of God flowed in and through his life.

The difference in Peter and the other disciples was that they now had a new and deeper relationship with the Lord than they'd ever known. When Jesus sent the Holy Spirit into their lives, it meant He would never leave them or forsake them. Through the Holy Spirit, He would now guide their lives from within.

WHAT COMES FIRST

Megan was a brilliant student in college, earning honors in her biology degree as well as being an athlete. When she first came to our church, she had no religious background. She was from a good family, but not a Christian one. As she was being drawn to the Lord, everything about Christianity was new to her.

One night she came over to our home to talk with my wife and me (Mel). She arrived with two pages of questions she wanted answered. As I looked over the long list, I was impressed by her sincere desire to know truth. But I sensed I needed to challenge her to enter into a relationship with the Lord and then allow *Him* to answer her questions.

"Megan," I said, "you're trying to run before you can walk. You want to know the deep things of God before you've responded to the simple things. In fact, you'll never understand the relationship with God until you first enter the relationship. You're trying to be a mature Christian before you've been born."

As I talked with her, I could see the Spirit of God stirring in her heart. I shared with her the simple message of the gospel and then asked, "Do you sense in your spirit that what I've said is true?"

She said, "With all my heart."

"Then respond to what you *do* know," I urged her, "and give your life to Jesus Christ. Once you enter a relationship with Him, He'll give you the gift of the Holy Spirit to help you know the deep things of God."

It was like a light turned on. Megan immediately smiled and said she wanted to enter the relationship. So my wife and I prayed with her and witnessed the moment she was born again into the family of God.

The next week at church, Megan rushed up to me and said, "I used to read the Bible, and it made no sense. But now it's alive. I'm understanding it. You were right! The relationship with Christ was what I needed, and I sense His Spirit within me."

What Megan discovered is foundational for all of us: the relationship must come first. Don't try to understand the deep things of God without first being born again of the Spirit of God. Don't try to do great things for God without first being empowered by the Spirit of God. Your entire Christian life is a by-product of this relationship.

Jesus promised us a Helper—the gift of the Holy Spirit who would dwell in us. If the Spirit isn't in you, and if you're not walking in step with Him, you cannot experience God in His fullness.

FOR EACH AND ALL

The empowerment that Peter and the apostles experienced in Acts is for every believer, not just those who are "called into the ministry." The fullness of the Spirit is not reserved for the spiritual giant or the supersaint. No, the Spirit is given to sinners and failures who have learned to repent and have come to experience the cleansing blood of Jesus over their lives. The Spirit is given to those who recognize their need and cry out for God's help.

All who believe God's good news of salvation and commit their lives to Jesus Christ will receive the same Holy Spirit who indwelt the Son of God. The power demonstrated in His life—and in His resurrection from the dead—was the power of the Holy Spirit working within Him. That same power is available to all believers. As Paul said, "If the Spirit of Him who raised Jesus from the dead dwells in you, He who raised Christ from the dead will also give life to your mortal bodies through His Spirit who dwells in you" (Romans 8:11). This is an amazing truth that we must not move past too quickly: the powerful Holy Spirit who worked in Jesus' life is the same Spirit who works in *us.*

That's what we need to hear today! Resurrection power is found in the Holy Spirit, the Holy Spirit is found in every believer, and the degree to which we walk in the Spirit's fullness and power is the degree to which our lives will impact the world around us. "'Not by

might nor by power, but by My Spirit,' says the LORD of hosts"
(Zechariah 4:6).

NO WALK, NO GIFT

We've often heard people confess to being far from the Lord—while
in the next breath they tell us what their spiritual gift is! They know
they're not walking in the Spirit, yet they want to be involved in the
church because of their perceived spiritual gifts. Such a disconnect
between the Spirit and His gifts is impossible.

We must understand a simple principle: *if you do not walk in the
Spirit, you do not have a spiritual gift.* Apart from the Spirit, whatever
"gifts" we display can be only our natural talents, drawing attention
to self.

Believers often ask each other (or themselves), "What's your
spiritual gift?" The true answer to that question is this: the *Holy
Spirit* is the gift. He Himself is the indispensable gift of God in your
life. He's the third Person of the Trinity, just as needful in your life
as the other two.

This singular gift of the Spirit is God's full provision for our
lives. In the Spirit, the Lord has given us everything we need: He's
the open door to heaven's wisdom, and He's our source of power for
every assignment. His presence within us is the crowning work of
God's great salvation toward those who believe—*for the glory of God.*

Peter said in Acts 2:38, "Repent, and let every one of you be

[handwritten margin note:] Gifts are not related to maturity.

baptized in the name of Jesus Christ for the remission of sins; and you shall receive the gift of the Holy Spirit." Everyone who repents and turns to Jesus as Lord and Savior will receive the incredible gift of the Holy Spirit, a gift of relationship with God.

GOD'S PURPOSE FOR THE GIFT

Spiritual gifts are bestowed on believers according to the purposes of God and are distributed according to the sovereign wisdom of God. Our spiritual gifts never belong to us; they're an expression of the Holy Spirit doing the Father's will through us.

Never forget that the Spirit is given to each one to equip us to do *God's* will, not our will. As Paul said, "One and the same Spirit works all these things, distributing to each one individually *as He wills*" (1 Corinthians 12:11). You cannot convince the Holy Spirit to do what He doesn't want to do, and He *always* wants to do the Father's will. If you're living outside His will, it's impossible to function according to any spiritual gift you may think you have, for you aren't walking in the Spirit. The Spirit manifests Himself in our lives to accomplish God's purpose and bring glory to God.

We learn much about God's purpose in giving the Holy Spirit when we ponder this profound statement from Paul: "The manifestation of the Spirit is given to each one for the profit of all" (1 Corinthians 12:7). Each phrase in that verse is important; each must be applied to your life.

The manifestation of the Spirit means that the Spirit will reveal *Himself* and His activity in you. Are you ready for Him to do that? Are you looking for Him and expecting Him to do His work? Be assured, He's ready to accomplish the Father's purposes in your life.

Paul also said the Holy Spirit would manifest Himself "to each one." Nobody is overlooked. *You* have received the gift of the Holy Spirit, and He'll manifest Himself in *your* life. No believer is left out, for the gift of the Spirit is the essence of what it means to be born again.

We hear people complaining about the talents and skills they lack, then concluding, "I don't have anything to offer God." That's likely true, but what does it have to do with the Holy Spirit working in your life? When God's Spirit is present, it doesn't matter what *you* can or cannot do. If you're lacking in natural talent, thank God that you're the perfect vessel for Him to show Himself powerful in and through your life. Listen to His promise: "My grace is sufficient for you, for My strength is made perfect in weakness" (2 Corinthians 12:9). In your weakness, He is strong. *You* are the person in whom He can do His best work, and He'll get all the glory.

The final part of Paul's statement about the Spirit in 1 Corinthians 12:7 is especially crucial: "for the profit of all." There's a corporate dimension to everything God does in your life. Every gift He has given is to be shared within the life of His people. If we aren't actively building up the body, we aren't functioning as God desires. The Holy Spirit will always seek to build the unity of the body, a unity that's precious in the heart of God. So don't run off and try to serve God on your own, but get involved with the people of God. For that's where the Spirit does His best work!

Hear it once more: the Holy Spirit Himself is God's gift to you. The same Holy Spirit who manifested Himself in the life of Jesus and in the early believers has been sent to work through you. If you open your life to Him, He'll manifest His power in your life. Don't bypass the relationship and try to experience the power. *First the relationship, then the power.*

EXPOSING THE EXCUSES

As a pastor, I (Mel) love to see the process that occurs when God is shaping a life for His purposes. I saw it particularly when I was teaching a series of messages in our church about the gift of the Holy Spirit for every believer and how He's present to equip us for anything God asks us to do. After the series was over, a man in his early fifties came to me and said, "Thanks, Pastor. You just destroyed every excuse I had for not getting involved."

This man had spent a lot of energy over the years explaining why he was unable to obey God: he wasn't well educated, he was divorced, he was shy, and he didn't have all the abilities he saw in other people in leadership. He was just an unskilled layperson. How could God use him to do anything?

He finally realized that those excuses were the same as telling the Holy Spirit, "You are not able to work through me." God's Spirit *not able*? Impossible! The problem had nothing to do with the ability of the Spirit; it had everything to do with the disobedience of the servant.

As a result of this realization, this man stepped out in faith and obeyed the Lord "beyond his ability." Today he's being used by God as a significant member of the body, and he has been blown away by what the Spirit has enabled him to do.

THE SPIRIT IS SPEAKING...

If the Holy Spirit at this time is impressing truth upon your spirit, you must respond immediately. This moment will not merely *lead* you to an encounter with God; this moment *is* an encounter with God.

What is God's Spirit saying to you? Are you seeking on your own to do good things for God, or do you allow Him to do His will through you? Do you need to make major adjustments in how you relate to the Holy Spirit?

It's amazing how many people have neglected the Holy Spirit, as if He's an afterthought of God. Have you neglected the person of the Holy Spirit in your life? If so, repent and ask Him to forgive you for relegating Him to a position much less than He deserves. Recognize the gift of Pentecost as a daily reality—and live with the expectation that the Holy Spirit is currently working in your life.

May you come to know and experience the gift of the Holy Spirit in all His fullness. And may you open your life for Him to teach you, lead you, and work through you for His glory.

CHAPTER 6

SHAPED FOR SERVICE

The Spirit of the Lord GOD is upon Me, because the
LORD has anointed Me to preach good tidings to the
poor; He has sent Me to heal the brokenhearted, to
proclaim liberty to the captives, and the opening of the
prison to those who are bound.

—ISAIAH 61:1

When you consider how Pentecost relates to your life, remember God's purpose for sending the Holy Spirit. As you read about the early disciples in the New Testament, ask yourself why God sent them the Spirit. And why does He send the Spirit to believers today?

Simply this: He has a mission. In sending the Spirit, God is at the same time giving an assignment. For unless there's an assignment, there's no need for the gift of Pentecost.

Because God has a purpose for your life, He has sent you the Holy Spirit to enable you to fulfill the assignment He wants to

Sanctification + transformation require the gift.

accomplish through you. God isn't looking for proven leaders; He's looking for those who have hearts that are pure and responsive, and then He equips them by His Spirit to be leaders. So hear this carefully: The Lord is looking not for the talented, but for the obedient. He's looking not for the skilled, but for those who are sensitive to His Spirit.

LAUGHED AT BY THE SPIRIT

A few years ago, I (Mel) experienced a weekend that was very unusual. The strangeness began when I received a call on my cell phone on Saturday morning. Because of an emergency situation, my dad needed me to cover for him and speak at a major pastors' conference in New York on Monday. This phone conversation distracted me from what I was doing at the time, and I accidentally filled my diesel pickup truck with gasoline.

Not good. I realized my blunder immediately, so I walked to a nearby store and bought them out of gas cans. The sight of me siphoning gas out of the truck must have been suspicious to everyone driving by.

But that wasn't the end of the strangeness. After preaching in our church on Sunday morning, I rushed to the airport. The plan was to spend the night in Chicago, then fly on to New York the next morning. Once I got to Chicago, it took me forever to find the hotel because of airport construction. I finally arrived there—late, tired, and hungry.

Since going to the conference had been a last-minute decision for me, I hadn't yet prepared what I would speak about. I decided to get a little study time before turning in. That's when I realized I'd forgotten my Bible. Here I was going to a pastors' conference to speak, and I didn't even have a Bible. I considered stealing the Gideon Bible from the hotel room and making a donation, but I didn't think God could honor a sermon preached from a stolen Bible.

Since I had an early flight the next morning, I decided to get to bed. That's when I discovered I'd also forgotten to bring my electric razor. That may not sound like a big deal, but if you use an electric razor, you understand my problem. My skin wasn't prepared for the free plastic razor the hotel supplied. Talk about being "washed in the blood"! My face the next morning was covered with razor nicks. Desperately trying to stop the bleeding, I left the hotel with little pieces of tissue on my face.

Eventually I arrived in New York to speak to the pastors at the meeting. I was told ahead of time that I would also be allowed to attend a special luncheon meeting the following day for ambassadors to the United Nations, and the man in charge would meet me that evening after the pastors' conference concluded. He did so, and he said to me, "While you were preaching tonight, the Lord told me that you're to speak to the ambassadors tomorrow at the United Nations." He added, "You'll have forty-five minutes to speak. This will be the largest gathering of ambassadors we've had at such an event, and many are from Muslim countries and aren't Christians. You can speak freely about your faith and talk about the Scripture, but protocol requires that you do not read from the Bible." Well, that at least was no issue for me, since I'd forgotten my Bible!

I obviously hadn't prepared to speak to the UN ambassadors, and it seemed like there was no time in the schedule to get ready. I was too exhausted that night and fell asleep. The morning began with an early breakfast, a train ride into Grand Central Station, a walk through pouring rain to an office building one block from the UN headquarters, and one hour to study before going to the meeting.

At the United Nations, we went through the security-check process to enter the building, then further security checks to access a floor reserved for ambassadors. We entered a fancy dining room where a string quartet was playing, and I immediately began to meet others who were coming in the door.

The first man I met was the head of the General Assembly, who said, "I'm looking forward to this lunch. We've been talking all morning about antiterrorism, and it will be nice to sit back and listen to what you have to say."

I thought to myself, *What* am *I going to say? I'm curious to hear as well!*

We sat down for lunch, eight to a table. I was tired, nervous, and felt way out of place. When I looked down at the food being served, I had no idea what it was. I was so edgy that I flipped a large leaf of lettuce onto my lap. I was trying to look calm, cool, and collected, but mentally I was a mess. *What am I doing here?* I asked myself. *Why did I agree to this? The only reason I'm here is that Dad couldn't come.*

Then it happened. I think the Holy Spirit within me started to laugh. Have you ever been laughed at by the Holy Spirit? I sensed Him saying, *Do you still think this is about* you? *You can't even shave! You're from a small church in a small town in Canada, and nobody here even knows you.*

Then He said, *The only reason you're speaking at the United Nations is because I put you here.* Then came this verse: "Now when they bring you to the synagogues and magistrates and authorities, do not worry about how or what you should answer, or what you should say. For the Holy Spirit will teach you in that very hour what you ought to say" (Luke 12:11–12).

I also remembered the e-mail sent to me that morning from the men in my church, who wanted me to know they were praying for me. Immediately an overwhelming peace covered me. When I got up to speak, it was as if I stood back and listened to myself. The leader later told me he couldn't remember the group being so engaged by a speaker.

The Lord wanted to do something with those ambassadors that day, and He chose to do it through my life. I remember thinking as I flew home from that trip, *With God, nothing is impossible.*

Why do I tell you that story? I want you to know that if God can use a simple person like me to do His will, He can use anybody.

POWER FOR A PURPOSE

That's what Pentecost is all about, just as we've seen in Acts: God can take simple men like the disciples and make the world marvel.

Some will object, "But that was with men like Peter and John. I don't have their courage." Courage? Are you talking about these guys before Pentecost or after? Think of Peter. Before Pentecost, he was full of bold talk but no action. He told Jesus, "Though all the others deny you, I'll go with you to prison and to death!" He couldn't have been more wrong. And who was it that prompted Peter's shameful denial of his Lord after Jesus was arrested? A soldier? A powerful religious leader? No, it was only a young servant girl.

It's that way with all the great leaders in the Bible: we remember mostly the climax of their lives and what they did *after* receiving the gift of the Spirit.

We think of Gideon as a fearless warrior who led a small group of three hundred volunteers to destroy an army of one hundred twenty thousand. But when God called him, Gideon was hiding from the enemy for fear they would steal his food. "O my Lord," he protested, "how can I save Israel? Indeed my clan is the weakest in Manasseh, and I am the least in my father's house" (Judges 6:15). Yet God had a purpose to fulfill through his life, and so as Scripture says, "The Spirit of the LORD came upon Gideon" (Judges 6:34).

We think of David as a powerful king who killed the giant and

ruled over Israel. But when God called him, he was a young shep-
herd boy, so insignificant that nobody thought to have him join his
brothers when the prophet Samuel came at God's command to
anoint one of them as king. Yet God had a purpose to fulfill through
David's life, so as Scripture says, "The Spirit of the LORD came upon
David" (1 Samuel 16:13).

We also think of the Old Testament prophets who boldly stood
up to evil in their day, fearlessly proclaiming God's truth to those
who were caught up in their wealth and power and comfort. But the
prophet Amos is typical of what these men were in and of themselves: when Amos was called by God, he was a simple sheep breeder
from Tekoa and a migrant laborer who worked picking fruit. Yet
God had a purpose to fulfill through the lives of all His prophets.
Therefore they could say, as the prophet Micah did, "Truly I am full
of power by the Spirit of the LORD" (Micah 3:8).

CALLED TO CHRISTLIKENESS

On the Day of Pentecost, when Peter quoted God's words spoken by
the prophet Joel—"I will pour out My Spirit on all flesh" (Joel
2:28)—the people were "cut to the heart" as Peter preached. They
cried out, "What shall we do?" Peter's answer: "Repent...and you
shall receive the gift of the Holy Spirit. For the promise is to you
and...as many as the Lord our God *will call*" (Acts 2:37–39).

God has also called you. He has sent you. And He has given you the Holy Spirit because He has a purpose for your life. Remember again: it's the Lord's purpose, not yours. The Holy Spirit was sent to help you achieve *God's* purposes, not your dreams. And if you aren't willing to do His purposes, the Holy Spirit cannot work in you or through you.

We'll look further at spiritual gifts, but first we need to talk about holy character. The Spirit is sent to equip us for an assignment, but assignment is always based upon character. If you have small character, you'll be given a small assignment. If you have great character, you'll be given a great assignment.

The Holy Spirit's first assignment is that of pointing you to the Lord Jesus. He's shaping your character to be like Christ's. He'll do whatever it takes to make you Christlike in all areas of your life. He'll take your childlike faith and stretch you to trust Him with your very life. He'll take your selfish heart and mold it to be sacrificial in every way. He'll take your pride and strip you down to absolute humility. He'll take your secret sins and expose them so you might be made holy. He'll take your life of ease and show you the hard road of complete and total dependence. The Holy Spirit wants to create within you holy character.

Our challenge to you is this: let Him do His work! So often we want a great assignment, but we resist His work that can give us great character.

EVEN FOR JESUS

This character-building work was even a part of the Lord Jesus' life. Notice how Luke indicated this truth during the time when Jesus was launching His ministry:

- The Spirit "descended...upon Him" for the assignment of redemption (3:22).
- Jesus "was led by the Spirit into the wilderness" to be tempted by Satan for forty days (4:1–2).
- The Spirit led Him back to Galilee to preach: "Jesus returned in the power of the Spirit" (4:14).
- Jesus identified and proclaimed the purpose of the Holy Spirit's coming upon Him: "The Spirit of the LORD is upon Me, because He has anointed Me to preach the gospel to the poor; He has sent Me to heal the brokenhearted, to proclaim liberty to the captives and recovery of sight to the blind, to set at liberty those who are oppressed" (4:18).
- His Spirit-led ministry brought Him into opposition— people hated Him and tried to kill him (4:28–29).

Can you see how the Spirit led Jesus into trying times so He could shape the Lord's life?

The most startling and profound statement about this process in the Lord's life is found in Hebrews 5:8: "He learned obedience by the things which He suffered." Think about what such a statement implies in *your* life. What will it mean for the Holy Spirit to make you Christlike? What must the Holy Spirit do to build great character in you? Every great Christian we know—without exception—has a testimony of suffering. Knowing this, do you still want a great assignment from the Lord?

Are you willing for the Holy Spirit to build into your life great character? Do you see why we must talk to you about Holy Spirit *character* before discussing Holy Spirit *gifts*?

In his book *Heaven's Throne Gift*, Christian author James A. Stewart wrote,

> Many want the Spirit's power but not the Spirit's purity. The Holy Spirit does not rent out His attributes. His power is never separated from His glorious Self.

The Holy Spirit's power is best channeled through a holy person's life. Whereas forgiveness of sin is immediate, building character takes time. As you allow the Holy Spirit to lead you, He'll teach you the holy life.

HITTING THE WALL

Just as the Spirit led Jesus into the wilderness, the Spirit led me (Mel) into a wilderness. But it took a while.

My first five years in the pastorate were great. God seemed to bless

(handwritten margin note: Beyond the wind suffering of life?)

my ministry in every way. In fact, things were going so well, I couldn't understand why some pastors seem to struggle so much. Subconsciously, I almost thought they must be unspiritual. After all, if you just loved God and loved His people, shouldn't everything work out great?

Then I hit the wall. My wife and I experienced the most painful year of our lives. Gina had emergency surgery that required a lengthy process of physical healing. Meanwhile we learned that our daughter had cerebral palsy, and the pain of that discovery was almost unbearable. During this same period, when our emotions were severely strained, some people in our church acted in an ungodly way and hurt us deeply.

Right in the middle of our personal pain, the church, which was still young and fragile, began to struggle. We had a lot of new believers we'd led to the Lord, but not many mature ones. There was also a group of disgruntled Christians who had come from another church. Suddenly we found ourselves in a major struggle.

For the first time in my life, I became anxious. In fact, I didn't like going to church because I knew it was full of problems and I didn't have the energy to deal with them anymore. We were in a dark valley—and it hurt.

I remember sitting with Gina in the living room of our home and saying, "This has been the most difficult year of our lives, but it may just prove to be our most profitable year. God has chosen to teach us some things that He knows we need to learn, things that will impact the rest of our lives."

The Lord shaped us during that time in ways far deeper than we ever expected. He helped us understand how to walk with Christ in a dark time. He helped us fathom God's people in a way we never knew before. He gave us tenderness for struggling churches and struggling pastors. In fact, since that time, God has given us the opportunity to come alongside many hurting pastors and struggling churches.

If you want great character, there's a wilderness to enter; there's a valley to pass through. It's in those times that the Holy Spirit can show you Christ more clearly than at any other time in your life. In the process, you become more Christlike in character.

DON'T BE A MAVERICK

At the conclusion of the account of Paul's conversion on the way to Damascus in Acts 9, we read this:

> Immediately he preached the Christ in the synagogues, that He is the Son of God. Then all who heard were amazed.... Saul increased all the more in strength, and confounded the Jews who dwelt in Damascus, proving that this Jesus is the Christ. (verses 20–22)

Isn't that just like the Paul we've come to know? Gloriously saved and profoundly impacted by the Spirit, he preached with insight and power. But the Jews in Damascus plotted to kill him, and Paul had to escape at night over the city wall in a large basket lowered by his friends.

With excitement about joining God's people in Jerusalem in serving the Lord, Paul traveled there, where "he spoke boldly in the name of the Lord Jesus" (9:29). But at first the disciples at the mother church in Jerusalem "were all afraid of him" (9:26). And once again, the local Jews "attempted to kill him" (9:29), and Paul had to make his escape.

Paul was on a rough road. The Holy Spirit would be taking him on a journey to develop his character before he was ready for a great assignment. But at this critical point in Paul's life, God in His grace also chose to bring alongside him a friend and encourager named Barnabas.

You'll find that one of the ways the Holy Spirit builds your character is to take you through a challenging time, then bring others alongside you to give you strength. We believe in the role of the local church. Believers are interdependent. The Holy Spirit in you is also in those around you in the body of Christ, and the Holy Spirit uses them to help in your character-building process.

MORE PRAYERS, MORE ANSWERS

One of the biggest ways other believers help you is in praying for you. I (Mel) used to read Paul's request for prayer for boldness in

Ephesians 6:18–20 and think, *Why did Paul need to ask the church to pray for his boldness? He's the most courageous missionary who ever walked the earth!*

Then it dawned on me: Maybe that's exactly why he was so courageous. Other people were asking God to make him bold.

The Holy Spirit puts you into the lives of God's people, and He moves all of you together toward maturity in Christ. After all, didn't Jesus Himself have men around Him? It's true they were just frail men stumbling along, but Jesus wanted them by His side. And in His darkest moment, He chose to take some of them to Gethsemane, where His soul was grieved unto death. He wanted them to be there and to pray.

So don't be a spiritual maverick. Let the Holy Spirit shape your life through others in the body of Christ.

EASY TO DO THE HARD THINGS

Remember again, your spiritual gifts are for the particular assignment God has for you, and assignments are always based on your character. So don't seek gifts of the Spirit—seek the Holy Spirit in His fullness, and let Him prepare you for God's purposes.

Nineteenth-century New England Bible teacher A. J. Gordon once said,

It costs much to obtain the power of the Spirit: It costs self-surrender and humiliation and a yielding up of our most precious things to God; it costs the perseverance of long waiting, and the faith of strong trust. But when we are really in that power, we shall find this difference, that whereas before, it was hard for us to do the easiest things, now it is easy for us to do the hard things.

Let me say it once more: Don't seek the gifts—seek the Giver of gifts. Die to self and allow Him to fill your life. Give Him access to all that you are and ever will be. Then watch the Holy Spirit shape you into a vessel He can use for God's glory.

THE SPIRIT IS SPEAKING... *Do through you rather than do in you?*

Have you been more interested in what the Holy Spirit can *give* you than in what the Holy Spirit will *do* in you? He's at work, fulfilling the Lord's purposes in your life. So what is the Spirit doing in your life right now? What evidence do you see that He's shaping you under the guidance of the Lord?

Step back and look at your life from God's perspective. Where have you been? How did God rescue you from sin? In what ways has He clearly impacted your life? What has He impressed upon your heart that you can't seem to get away from?

Take a moment and thank the Spirit of God for what He has done in your life. Then ask Him to continue the process of shaping your life for service as you commit yourself to obey Him no matter the cost.

CHAPTER 7

GOD'S BEST IN YOUR LIFE

> Now when they saw the boldness of Peter and John, and
> perceived that they were uneducated and untrained
> men, they marveled. And they realized that they had
> been with Jesus.
>
> —ACTS 4:13

Anchor this truth in your mind: the gift of the Holy Spirit is primarily about God and His work, not about you and your work.

Most of the discussions we hear today about spiritual gifts revolve around what people are good at doing or what people most like to do. That approach tends to be self-glorifying: if we operate only according to our talents and ability, we get the glory. But if we function according to the power of the Spirit, God gets the glory as others around us see Him at work. And God's goal is to reveal *Himself* to a watching world, not to showcase our achievements.

Great talents in this world may impress people, but they don't impress God. He is far beyond any human ability and is impressed by only one thing—faith. He understands human pride and our desire to be honored, and when God sees people humble themselves and turn to Him for help, He smiles. It's in and through their humble lives that He can do His best work.

Consider the centurion who put his faith in the Lord. Although the world admired him for his power and influence, he confessed to Jesus his own unworthiness, and he stated his full understanding that ultimate power was found in Jesus. "When Jesus heard it, He marveled, and said to those who followed, 'Assuredly, I say to you, I have not found such great faith, not even in Israel!'" (Matthew 8:10). Because the centurion *believed* in the name of Jesus, he experienced the power of Jesus in his life and family. The centurion's faith became a blessing: his life in relationship with Christ impacted those around him, and God got the glory.

You can put your trust in your ability, or you can put your faith in God. The choice is yours. When you rely on your own talents, you'll experience your best. But when you put your faith in God and allow His Spirit to work in you, you'll experience God's best.

YOUR BEST VERSUS GOD'S

In equipping us to do God's will, the Holy Spirit doesn't give us a talent, skill, or ability to use as we desire; He gives us *Himself*. Then

He accomplishes the Father's will through our lives. This alone makes possible our experience of the divine power that turns the world upside down. As the apostle Peter wrote in 2 Peter 1:3: "His divine power has given to us all things that pertain to life and godliness, through the knowledge of Him who called us by glory and virtue."

Too often we're content to serve God by giving our own greatest effort. What is that, however, compared to the power of the Holy Spirit? What does the world really need to see: what we can do or what God can do? The world doesn't need to see good people giving their best to God; they need to encounter *God* doing in and through us what only He can do!

How strange it must sound to God when we counsel others (or ourselves), "Just do your best. That's all that matters." Do we want to give the world our best or let the world experience God's best? To give only the best we have is to cheat the world of what could have been. If we're a blessing to the world, it's not because of what we can do for others but because we're filled with the Spirit of God whereby we've become a channel of His blessing.

Living by the Spirit's power doesn't mean we should ignore our God-given abilities and talents. But we must never assume those talents are the only areas in which we can serve. We'll say more later about how we use our natural talents, but first we need to expose the myth that our natural talents are the same as spiritual gifts. They may, in fact, be worlds apart.

MISSING OUT ON SEEING GOD

When it comes to serving God, we tend to evaluate what we're good at and what we like to do, then serve according to our ability. We figure out what talents we have, assume that these are our spiritual gifts, then offer them to God.

This, in fact, is what others usually encourage us to do—to recognize where we're proficient and what we like to do, then serve according to our abilities, all the while asking God to bless our efforts. We never consider serving outside the areas of our strengths, and we can't imagine God asking us to do what we don't like to do. We look at our *self* to discover our assignment from God. How silly is that?

The result of this approach is that we don't need or rely on the Holy Spirit, because we're confident in our abilities. We're under the delusion that we have everything under control. The world, therefore, looks at the church and sees good people doing good things for God, but they don't see the power of God working through His people to accomplish *what only He can do.*

Think about it. If we were to serve according to our talents, why did Jesus send us the Holy Spirit? Why did Jesus tell the disciples to wait until the Spirit had come upon them? It was because *our best isn't good enough when it comes to kingdom work;* we need the Holy Spirit in our lives if we're going to be of use to God.

What's Hard for the Richly Talented

Among many startling statements Jesus made to people of His day was this one: "It is easier for a camel to go through the eye of a needle than for a rich man to enter the kingdom of God" (Matthew 19:24). This was an astounding assertion that went against everything the people had been taught; they'd always assumed wealth was a sign of God's blessing. But Jesus knew that wealth causes people to feel self-sufficient and can lead them away from God. Rich people may never know how to walk by faith and experience the provision of God, for they already have everything they need, and they rely on their own abilities to obtain whatever else they may want.

The same is true with those who are blessed with many natural talents. It's easier for a camel to go through a needle's eye than for someone with great talents to be used in the kingdom of God, for this person will be tempted to rely on natural abilities rather than the power of the Holy Spirit. He or she may even begin to confuse abilities with God's enabling Holy Spirit. And once a person's talents become a substitute for the work of the Holy Spirit, that person is of no use to God.

Don't get me wrong: God can use our talents. But never forget that He can also use our weaknesses. There are many ways God can get glory from our lives. Sometimes He'll enhance and sanctify our natural abilities and character qualities, while at other times He'll use

a person in ways that don't correspond to anything previously seen
in that person's life.

The Danger of Spiritual Inventories *Precisely right.*

One of the ways we're sometimes tempted to operate according to
natural talents instead of by the Spirit is through various tests known
as spiritual gift inventories. These tests have become popular, but
they can be confusing for many because of their inherent limitations.
If a non-Christian took such a test, then took it again a few months
later after becoming a Christian, it would probably produce the
exact same results. Yet why should we now call something a spiritual
gift when it would have been viewed as nothing more than a natural
talent only months earlier?

Think of it this way. Are there non-Christians who are gifted
musically? Are there non-Christians who are gifted teachers or gifted
motivational speakers? Yes, the lost world around us has many such
gifted people. But when those same people become Christians, why
would we automatically think of those talents as spiritual gifts when
they were present even before the Holy Spirit entered their lives?
These people had those abilities before they had the Holy Spirit.

Taking a spiritual gift inventory can help you understand where
you're strong and where you're weak. It can even help identify how
God has used you since you've become a Christian. But it shouldn't

be used as a guide for how God desires to use you in the future, for God's purposes are based upon *His* strengths, not yours alone. He may choose to take you into areas of service in which you're naturally weak in order to reveal His strength and bring glory to Himself. He may ask you to serve in an area that's uncomfortable for you, just so you can know the joy of His presence working through you. He might even take you into a place where, based upon your natural inclinations, you would never have imagined yourself. But once you're there, you can't imagine anything better for your life.

One of the dangers of relying on a spiritual gift inventory is that you'll be tempted to trust the test results and not turn to God to seek His perspectives about your giftedness. After all, why spend time seeking after God when you can take a test and get immediate results? Why trust your own walk with God when somebody else has done the work for you? You can be sure that God loves the time and attention you give to being in His presence. What He's after is not quick results but a lifelong relationship. He loves for you to cry out to Him and learn to be sensitive to His Spirit in your life.

Another danger with these inventories is that you may lock in your gifts and identify your field of service and therefore not be free to follow Christ in a new assignment. Too often people "discover" their spiritual gifts, then put on blinders that keep them from seeing anything outside their identified field of service. Our service to God shouldn't be a result of a written test; it should flow from a dynamic relationship with our living Lord whereby He guides our life day by day.

IN OUR WEAKNESS HE IS STRONG

The New Testament keeps reminding us: "The Christian life is not about you. It's about what God can do through you." Consider these words of the apostle Paul:

> For you see your calling, brethren, that not many wise according to the flesh, not many mighty, not many noble, are called. But *God has chosen the foolish things of the world* to put to shame the wise, and *God has chosen the weak things of the world* to put to shame the things which are mighty; and *the base things of the world and the things which are despised God has chosen, and the things which are not,* to bring to nothing the things that are, that no flesh should glory in His presence. (1 Corinthians 1:26–29)

Remember once more: when good people are giving their best talents to God, what the world sees and experiences is only the best *they* have, not the best *God* has for them.

People usually aren't all that impressed by our talent anyway; they have their own talents. But people marvel when they see an ordinary person doing extraordinary things in the power of the Holy Spirit. You can take a test and discover your personality traits; these are very helpful to know. You can take a test and clarify your strengths and weaknesses; this too is helpful information. But the work of the Holy Spirit is something no man-made test can capture.

Listen carefully here: the reason we're often sidetracked on this point is that it's so much easier to simply do what we're good at than it is to walk with God and obey Him when He asks us to do what we're unable to do in our own strength. That kind of obedience requires a relationship that's close enough to identify His will, a faith that's strong enough to trust His will, and a heart that's humble enough to submit to His will.

God may well ask you to do something you're not good at. He will often ask you do something you don't want to do. So if you intend to serve Him only according to your aptitudes and desires, you'll miss most of what He wants to do in your life. He'll use your abilities—but He's by no means limited by them!

Not a Job, but a Relationship

It's interesting to many that I (Henry) have served in churches as a minister to youth, minister of music, minister of education, and senior pastor, and I have also served as the president of a Bible college, a missionary, a conference speaker, and an author. So what is my spiritual gift? *The Holy Spirit. He* has enabled me to serve the

Lord in many different places, while giving me many different abilities along the way. What an adventure life becomes when the Holy Spirit is free to use your life according to the Lord's good pleasure and not your limited abilities.

Many times I look around in amazement at what God is doing through my life. And in those times I remember how important it is to keep my relationship with the Lord a priority. If He can take a shy boy from a small town in Canada and thrust him into places of influence among world leaders, He can use anybody.

It's not about what you bring to God but what He brings to you. And since He gave you the gift of Pentecost, every day is an adventure of divine magnitude.

Better than Knowing Yourself

So what about our natural talents and past experience? Will God use them, or will He always use us in areas where we're naturally weak?

God created you with your unique abilities, and He *does* want to use them. But He's far more concerned that you know *Him* than that you know your abilities. The world tells us to affirm self, but God tells us to deny self. Your identity and self-worth are found not in your abilities, but in your relationship to Christ.

We love to be in control. That's our nature—our fallen nature, that is. But we were created for a relationship with our Creator whereby *He* is in control. Ever since that relationship was torn apart by sin, we struggle to trust Him, for we don't know Him as we ought. It's much easier to put our faith in our ability, for we know our limitations and what we can accomplish.

We know in our head what the Bible teaches, but we have a hard time putting God's truth into practice. In many cases, we're theologically conservative believers but practical atheists. We struggle to live out what we say we believe. The life and the belief system don't match. But when it comes to theological matters, our goal isn't intellectual excellence but the deepest experience of all that God has purposed for our lives, based on theology that we know to be true. Therefore the only way to experience the Spirit working in our lives is to trust and obey.

To trust in God, we have to know Him intimately. It's not that we aren't aware of how much God can do; we just aren't living in a relationship with Him where we're confident He'll do all that much in our own lives. As a result, many Christians trust their own experience over the truth of God's Word. That's why the Holy Spirit continually points us to the Lord. That's why His greatest task is to help us know and experience a personal relationship with God.

When we do obey, however, God can accomplish more through us in six days than we could do in sixty years with our best efforts alone. In fact, without the Spirit working through our lives, everything we do is dead works. Jesus wasn't exaggerating when He said, "I am the vine, you are the branches. He who abides in Me, and I in him, bears much fruit; for *without Me you can do nothing*" (John

15:5). We rarely consider that God gave us His Spirit because "self" could never accomplish the assignment He has for us. Only through His Spirit are we equipped for service.

[handwritten margin note: This is common language. Does God have an assignment for everyone? Is this a bossy employee relationship?]

DO THE IMPOSSIBLE?

So an important question to ask is this: will God ever ask you to do something you aren't even able to do?

Yes, all the time! God wants to use your life in a whole new world of opportunity beyond your areas of competence and experience. Hence, the gift of the Holy Spirit.

So never put limits on how God can use your life. Obey almighty God and trust that He knows what He's doing in your life. Don't look at your abilities and natural talents alone and serve only in the areas you feel competent. If you do, you'll eliminate yourself from significant arenas of service.

All the way through the Bible, Old Testament and New, God has done mighty works through His people. We know this from historical observation. But for some reason we don't expect Him to do mighty works today, especially in our own lives or church.

We are servants, and Christ is our master. The servant never tells the master what he or she wants to do for him; the servant simply obeys the master. Can you imagine the master giving an order to the servant and the servant replying, "Sorry, that isn't my gift"? That would be ridiculous, and even more so when you realize that it's

Christ giving the orders. He'll never ask you to do anything that He won't also enable you to do.

Consider Jesus' question to the disciples in Matthew 16:15: "Who do you say that I am?" Think about that. If He were to ask you the same question, how would you respond? If your response was similar to Peter's—"You are the Christ, the Son of the living God" (verse 16)—Jesus would then ask you, "How much of Me are you experiencing in your life? Are you content to learn about Me, or do you want to experience in your life what I've just revealed to you?"

In Peter's response to that question from Jesus, he was saying, "You are the promised Messiah, the hope of our nation, the only Savior of the world, and the Son of the living God who holds all power in His hands." In Christ all the fullness of the Godhead dwells, and all authority in heaven and earth has been given to Him. So if you truly believe He's now seeking to live out His life of fullness through you, where's the evidence?

Is the presence of Christ only a doctrinal statement for you? Or is it a practical experience of His living in you through the power of the Holy Spirit? God's Word says that He's the only Savior of the world. Do you believe that? If you did, you would make sure every person had the opportunity to hear the gospel. We're called to take the gospel to every person, because there's no other way to God. And the Savior has come to your life to involve you in His great plan of salvation.

So we must learn to seek God's will and obey Him no matter how difficult and uncomfortable the assignment and no matter how high the cost—knowing we're called to accomplish those tasks not according to our own capacity, but according to the fully enabling power of the Holy Spirit.

THE SPIRIT IS SPEAKING...

To be of use to God, we must take our eyes off self and look into the eyes of the Lord. Don't consider what you can bring to Him; think about what He has already given to you. Jesus is active and at work in this world, and He gave you the gift of the Holy Spirit so you could join Him in that activity. And when you walk with Him, full of the Spirit, you'll have a significant role in bringing people to salvation.

Are you content merely to give the world your best? Or do you want people to experience the power of the Holy Spirit when they encounter your life? What a difference!

You must completely release your life to the work of the Spirit. Don't be afraid; don't hesitate. It's a decision that will turn your world upside down.

CHAPTER 8

TALENTED OR GIFTED?

For the kingdom of God is not in word but in power.

—1 CORINTHIANS 4:20

The great challenge of God is to turn His people from being self-centered to being God-centered. Our natural bent is to start with self and base our decisions on what we can accomplish. Instead, we need to start with God and simply respond to Him in obedience. Our response is based not upon our talents, but upon His assignment for our lives.

WITNESS TO A MIRACLE

I (Mel) enjoy sharing the gospel with those who've never heard it. I don't have a canned approach to witnessing. My strategy is to discover what God is doing in a person's life, reword from a biblical perspective what I've heard them say, and then help them take the next step in their response to God. I look to see what God is doing in their lives and join Him.

As I do this, normally my mind is sharp and quick to recall a Scripture, and I share it in a relational and natural way. But that wasn't the case one night when I went to see a couple who had visited our church. I'd just finished a very demanding day, and I was physically tired and mentally spent; I just wasn't sharp.

I usually take someone with me when I'm witnessing, so I had a seminary student along for the experience. When we came to the house, nobody answered the door when I rang the doorbell. Then I realized I was at the wrong house.

When we finally made it to the right house and were invited inside, the couple was timid and uneasy. As we sat around their kitchen table, I realized I'd forgotten my Bible. Everything seemed awkward and cold.

I asked about their religious background and what had drawn them to visit our church. As I listened to their story of drifting from one church to another without ever being involved in any of them, I realized how spiritually confused the wife was. She had been involved with Catholics, Lutherans, Pentecostals, Baptists, and others, with long periods of "nothing" in between.

"I have a lot of questions," she said.

"I'm sure you have a lot of questions," I replied, "especially with such a varied religious past. But before I answer them, can I ask you just one question? In all the churches you've visited, did anyone ever tell you how to become a Christian?"

"No," she said. "Nobody has ever told me that."

"Do you mind if I tell you?"

"Please," she replied eagerly. "I've always wanted to understand that."

So I launched into a presentation of the gospel. But remember, I wasn't at my best. I borrowed an old King James Bible the couple had and stumbled along to share with them. I have to be honest; this was probably the worst gospel presentation in the history of the world. In fact, it was so bad, I started to question it!

While I was turning the conversation from small talk to spiritual talk, the seminary student who was with me knew where I was going. As I presented the gospel, he had discreetly bowed his head and was praying for me. When he lifted his head, he was absolutely amazed. Tears were rolling down the woman's cheeks. She wasn't crying because of my terrible presentation; something was obviously touching her deep within. She moved past weeping to sobbing, and from sobbing to heaving. Her husband was stunned, not knowing what was happening to his wife. He ran for tissues and tried to comfort her.

As the scene unfolded before my eyes, I sensed the Holy Spirit say to me, *I'm trying to save this poor woman, so don't mess this up. Just help her to repent and ask Jesus into her life. Then stop talking!*

That's what I did. She prayed to receive Christ, and the husband recommitted his life to the Lord. Both of them committed to come forward in church the following Sunday.

As we walked out of the house, no more than thirty minutes after we'd arrived, we sat in the car stunned. I thought, *God was determined to save that woman in spite of our incompetence!*

Now, based upon that true story (and believe me, I wish I could say it was just a fabricated case study to make a point), would you say I have the gift of evangelism? After all, we were in and out in only thirty minutes (fifteen of which was small talk and cookies). The woman was left in a heap of tears as she prayed to receive Christ, and the man reawakened to his relationship with God and cried out for forgiveness and restoration. Another two people were added to our church membership.

So I *must* have the gift of evangelism, right? Or isn't it more accurate to say I have the gift of the Holy Spirit who fulfilled the Father's purpose through my life?

What happened that night? The Father purposed to do a work in this couple's lives. Christ sent me as a part of His body to share the gospel. And the Holy Spirit worked through me to bring them into a relationship with God.

I was available for the Holy Spirit to work through my life, and He did. What turned this couple's lives upside down was not my skilled approach to witnessing, but the power of the Holy Spirit. So what's most important: my skill as a witness or the presence of the Holy Spirit? Obviously it's the Holy Spirit's power that makes the difference. And that's true for everything we do in the kingdom of God.

THOSE WHOM GOD USES

Here's a typical scenario in our churches: The right person is being sought to serve as chairman of the finance committee, and the church turns immediately to someone such as a financially success-ful banker or businessperson. However, the church gives no thought to whether that person has even the faintest idea of how to walk by faith and trust in God. He or she then steps into the position and by all appearances manages the church's money well—so well that the church never experiences what God could have done if they had trusted more in Him.

Success in the world doesn't equate with success in the kingdom of God. In fact, it can often divert our praise away from God and onto the achievements of people. Every person who serves in the power of the Spirit will at the same time build up the body and bring glory to God.

Our tendency seems always to judge a person's usefulness to God in terms of external factors. But those whom everyone expects to succeed because of their apparent strengths or their great and nu-merous talents are more likely to fail in the work of God's kingdom. They're especially in danger if they listen to the press reports of how good they are.

But God, in choosing and calling His servants, focuses not on outward appearances but on their hearts and their walks with Him. Again, He looks not for natural leaders, but for those whose hearts are pure and whose faith is strong.

HUMILITY FIRST

My (Henry) father was a branch manager for a bank all my life. Fortunately, he was a Christian businessman with great spiritual integrity. He was one of the godliest men I've ever known. In contrast to many of his colleagues, he knew God and walked by faith. He helped finance small businesses not by the world's standards but by God's. He based his choices on character and potential good, often to the amazement of others. And God blessed not only his work at the bank but also the entire community.

I recall that he would often talk about the danger of choosing leaders based on natural skill rather than on spiritual integrity and maturity. He was very concerned about people and their impact upon God's work.

God *is* using men and women of great talent and ability, but when He does, the first assignment of the Holy Spirit is to bring humility. They must cease to compare themselves to others and instead measure themselves against almighty God. The Holy Spirit must deal with their self-image and replace it with the image of Christ. That's not an easy task.

But hear the word of the Lord: "On this one will I look: on him who is poor and of a contrite spirit, and who trembles at My word" (Isaiah 66:2). Therein is the key for every person who is used of God: a humble estimation of self and a reverent esteem for God. God's eyes are upon those who have a deep hunger for the Bible and prayer, for they know it leads to the way of life.

WHERE GOD LOOKS

Be assured that when God determines whether to use you in His work, He isn't on the lookout for someone talented, good-looking, well spoken of, or highly educated. He's searching above all for one whose heart is pure. When He finds that pure heart, He'll fill it with His Spirit and move through that person's life with power. "For the eyes of the LORD run to and fro throughout the whole earth, to give strong support to those whose heart is blameless toward him" (2 Chronicles 16:9, ESV).

This promise is given to every believer, for we all have the capacity to choose the master to whom we give our hearts. We've been "set free from sin" through Jesus Christ and are now "slaves of righteousness" (Romans 6:18).

Remember again Paul's words to the Corinthians about who and what God chooses to work through: "the foolish things of the world…the weak things of the world…the base things of the world and the things which are despised" (1 Corinthians 1:27–28). Paul could point to his own life in this regard, knowing he was "the least of the apostles"—unworthy even to be an apostle because of his past persecution of Christians (1 Corinthians 15:9). Yet God was gracious to use Paul mightily.

When God has a task that needs a laborer, He doesn't go looking for one who has the right gifts. He looks for one who has an obedient heart, so He can accomplish the task through that person and receive all the glory.

The late evangelist Roy Hession in his book *Be Filled Now!* made this startling statement:

> Someone has said, "The Spirit's fullness is not the reward of our faithfulness, but God's gift for our defeat." He was not given to the disciples in Acts 28 as the culmination and reward of their wonderful service, but in Acts 2 when they had proved themselves cowards, meeting behind barred doors.

It's true that our greatest point of weakness can at the same time become the opportunity for God to do His greatest work.

Remember the Lord's words to the prophet Samuel after sending him to find and anoint Israel's king? "The LORD does not see as man sees; for man looks at the outward appearance, but the LORD looks at the heart" (1 Samuel 16:7). Have you been looking at your "outward appearance" and your physical abilities as a gauge for your service to God? That isn't what the Lord is looking at. The Lord looks at your heart. What's the condition of your heart? Do you spend more time and effort honing your skills than you do seeking the Lord and deepening your relationship with Him?

ALL SO ORDINARY

There are many examples in the Bible of God using people who had no ability of their own to accomplish His purposes. Think again of Gideon. He was probably the last person anyone would have chosen to lead God's people into battle. God, however, saw him as a "mighty man of valor" (Judges 6:12)—even though, when the angel of the Lord came to him, Gideon was hiding from the enemy and threshing wheat in a winepress for fear they would steal his food.

When the Lord gave him an assignment, Gideon's response was honest: "O my Lord, how can I save Israel? Indeed my clan is the weakest in Manasseh, and I am the least in my father's house" (Judges 6:15). Gideon was right: he had no innate abilities that qualified him to lead people into battle. "But the Spirit of the LORD came upon Gideon" (6:34), and God's power was displayed through him and his men.

The result of Gideon's obedience? With three hundred men he defeated an army of one hundred twenty thousand. Impossible? For Gideon, yes. But not for God! Therefore the watching world gave glory to God, for only He could have given such a victory. The nations of the world did not fear the Israelites, but they did learn to fear the *God* of the Israelites.

Or think again of the prophet Amos. His book of prophecy in the Bible begins, "The words of Amos, who was among the sheep-breeders of Tekoa" (1:1). Amos was a nobody from an insignificant place and doing unremarkable work. He cared for sheep and worked in fruit orchards. What in his background qualified him to stand before the king and boldly pronounce God's word? Nothing. Yet Amos was greatly used of God for a special assignment as the Spirit enabled him.

Or think once more about Peter—only a fisherman, unpolished, rough, abrasive, and speaking the tongue of a commoner. Was he really able to lead the disciples, preach the first gospel sermon at Pentecost, stand in the temple courts defying the religious elite, and write words that would go down in Scripture? *Wrong question!* The right question is this: can the Holy Spirit work through an ordinary laborer named Peter? *Yes!* A thousand times yes!

GOD'S MAKEOVER

As you recall what God did through such men in Scripture, consider this: If Gideon had taken a spiritual gifts inventory to determine his future course of action, his chances for taking a job as a military general would be almost nil. If Amos had analyzed and charted his talents and abilities, he would not have stood before the king. If Peter had done the same, he wouldn't have become an apostle. Likewise, David would never have been king of Israel, Joseph wouldn't have ruled in Egypt, Nehemiah wouldn't have rebuilt the walls of Jerusalem, and Paul wouldn't have been a missionary.

If pursuing God's work depended on their own perceived abilities, most if not all of our heroes of the faith would never have become known. After evaluating their strengths and abilities, they most likely would have concluded they didn't have what it took to meet the awesome task before them. The assignment just didn't match their "gift set."

But today we view these people as champions of the faith—because we've seen the last chapter of their lives. If, however, you'd met them before their encounter with the Lord and their filling by the Spirit, you would have found them to be very unassuming people, quite ordinary, and often poor, weak, and insignificant.

"Extreme makeovers" have been popular on television, and seeing the before and after is often dramatic. But no Hollywood makeover can compare to the work of the Holy Spirit to transform a person's life. His specialty is using ordinary men and women in extraordinary ways.

THE RIGHT HEART

I (Mel) had to laugh when our church went through the process of electing new deacons. The congregation had made its nominations, and the chairman and I were interviewing the candidates. One particular candidate made a fascinating comment. With a look of bewilderment, he said, "But I don't *look* like a deacon!"

In his mind he saw a picture of someone wearing a nice suit, theologically educated, strait-laced, and clean-cut. This man, however, served in the police force, raced cars professionally, and didn't wear suits. In his mind, he didn't have the right gifts—but the church recognized that he had the right heart. He was a man of character. And the Lord can equip a man like that to do whatever the assignment requires of him.

GIFTED FOR AN ASSIGNMENT

Remember again, the Holy Spirit gives gifts to God's people so they can fulfill the assignment given them. No assignment, no need for the gift of the Holy Spirit. There are some who want to enjoy all the fruit of Pentecost without an assignment. But that isn't biblical. The whole purpose of Pentecost was to enable us to do His will.

Too many people want an experience without an assignment. They look at all the signs, wonders, and miracles, but they forget that these things accompany the assignment of God. The miracles have a purpose in the heart of God, and that purpose is not to satisfy our curious and egocentric nature. Yet we have a whole generation trying to tell us we can have the experience of Pentecost without an assignment. They've missed the whole point of Pentecost.

Do you want to be filled with the Holy Spirit? For what purpose? So you can enjoy Him? You will enjoy His presence in your life, but that's not the major purpose of Pentecost. Its major purpose is to give you heaven's full provision for fulfilling God's assignments in your life.

Think again of those early disciples, a group made up of ordinary people. After they had witnessed the Cross and the Resurrection, Jesus clearly told them to wait for the anointing from heaven. They hadn't yet experienced Pentecost, but they soon would. Receiving the Holy Spirit would be a necessity in their lives—just as it had been for Jesus. Before Jesus could fulfill the assignment given to Him, the Spirit came upon Him at His baptism. Likewise, the disciples had to have the Spirit come upon them before they could take on their assignment of sharing the gospel to a lost world.

What was true of Jesus and what was true of the disciples is also true of us. We need the Holy Spirit.

KINGDOM LIVING

One of the unique assignments God has given me (Henry) over the past several years is to walk alongside many of the top CEOs of America. Many of them have had a sudden compulsion to "seek first the kingdom of God and His righteousness" (Matthew 6:33), right in the midst of the business world. They realize that God has placed them in their positions of influence intentionally and that He desires to use their lives for kingdom purposes. As they see themselves as kingdom citizens first and businesspeople second, they begin to see the reign of God in the workplace.

All through His life, Jesus spoke of the kingdom of God. It was a high priority for Him. The reign and rule of God was first and foremost on His mind, and He allowed the Father to use His life to extend the kingdom. And since the Father was ruling through Jesus' life, the power of God was also present.

The same is true for us. Once people recognize that God wants to rule in their lives and express His power in the world in which He has placed them, everything looks different. It's no longer about "my" ability and determined efforts to change the world.

The rise or fall of the economy doesn't catch God off guard. Environmental issues aren't a mystery to the One who created all things. Natural disasters aren't a surprise that alter His plans. Though we're often perplexed by life's circumstances, God is not. As long as we walk with Him, He can use our lives to make a difference for eternity. And the Holy Spirit is present to gift us for such a time.

ADEQUATELY GIFTED

It's easy to size up your talents, or lack thereof, and excuse yourself from serving God. But you cannot be filled with the Spirit and ever have an excuse for disobedience. The Spirit is always able to complete what the Lord requires.

If you say, "I'm not an effective witness," what are you saying? Is not the Holy Spirit able to "convict the world of sin, and of righteousness, and of judgment" (John 16:8)? Though you've been reluctant to witness, are you willing to believe that the gift of the Spirit is able to effectively witness through your life? That's what He did with an ordinary man named Peter. On the Day of Pentecost, a fisherman preached, and three thousand souls were added to the kingdom that day. How did it happen? Peter was filled with the Spirit.

Never consider your past ability a gauge for future obedience. The most significant factor determining whether God can use your life is your relationship with Him. It's not what you can do *for* Him, but what you can do *with* Him. Challenging circumstances in life will create the opportunity that reveals your relationship with God. So keep your eyes on Christ, and He'll send the Holy Spirit to equip you for anything you encounter. Don't let the opinions of people shake you. Keep listening to the Lord, for He knows you best. And His words about your life are based upon what He's going to do *in* you.

The Spirit Is Speaking...

Do you sense that God wants to use your life, but you think you have nothing to offer Him? Don't merely look at what you have to offer the world; seek the heart of God and allow His Spirit to work through you. He'll touch the world in ways you could never touch it on your own. Perhaps the Holy Spirit has just invited you to a greater task in the work of God's kingdom.

If you're more concerned about the talents you don't possess than about those you do, you're of no use to God. But once you come to realize that God doesn't need your talents, you're ready for Him to express His power in your life.

He's looking for obedience. So take a moment to respond in prayer to what the Holy Spirit is saying to you today.

CHAPTER 9

FROM ORDINARY TO EXTRAORDINARY

And being assembled together with them, He commanded them not to depart from Jerusalem, but to wait for the Promise of the Father.

—ACTS 1:4

Sealing? ?
Anointing ? ?
Sanctifying ?

God sent the Holy Spirit on assignment. We must therefore ask these questions: In each of our lives, *what is that assignment*? Why was the Spirit sent to you, and what is He doing in your life? How do we get in step with Him and enjoy abundant life as Christ has promised?

As the Spirit reveals the will of the Father, we can then allow Him to accomplish it through our lives by the Spirit's enabling. Again, *equipping always follows the assignment*. The enabling power of the Holy Spirit *follows* the assignment, never precedes it. If we aren't willing to obey the Lord and do His will, there's no need for His gifts to us.

COMMANDMENT BEFORE COMMISSION

Have you noticed in the gospels that the Great Commandment was given before the Great Commission? It's true. Jesus said, "'You shall love the LORD your God with all your heart, with all your soul, and with all your mind.' This is the first and great commandment" (Matthew 22:37–38). This commandment is the basis for everything else you do. It will be impossible to serve God unless you first love Him. It's out of this relationship that we're enabled to serve Him. Once that's in place, we can "go therefore and make disciples of all the nations, baptizing them in the name of the Father and of the Son and of the Holy Spirit, teaching them to observe all things that I have commanded you" (Matthew 28:19–20).

God always works in that order. He's first concerned about our relationship to Him. Once we learn to walk with Him, we're able to hear His voice and obey. And as we make the adjustment to do His will, He then equips our lives to complete the assignment He has for us. You can count on it: God desires to bring you into the middle of His activity. It's then that our lives move from the ordinary to the extraordinary.

The disciples were mightily used of God but not until they had learned to walk with Jesus. In fact, it took the Lord almost three and a half years to prepare them. They had many adjustments to make in their lives, beginning with having to leave what they were doing to follow Jesus. They just knew they needed to be with Him, though they had no idea where their relationship with Him was going. But Jesus knew. He then fashioned their lives so they were ready to receive the commission to take the gospel to the ends of the earth.

Think about that for a moment. If the Lord took three and a half years to fashion the disciples before He gave them a major assignment, should you be asking for a significant place of service before you've learned to truly walk with Him? It may not be wise to ask for a major assignment on the front end. Perhaps you should instead ask Him to help you love God with all your heart, soul, and mind. And let Him take as long as He needs to prepare your heart for service.

Does God know you better than you know yourself? Does He know some area in your life that will hinder His ability to work through you? It may be your relationship to your parents. Perhaps He needs to deal with you in the area of materialism and finances. He may need to thoroughly address secret sins nobody else knows about. God knows about them—and He also knows that sin will destroy your ability to serve Him. Be careful not to run to the next assignment; run instead to Him. He'll give you an assignment when He knows you're ready.

We're not counseling you to be inactive or to in some way remove yourself from service in the church. The Lord will cause your life to be a blessing from the first day of salvation until the day you see Him face to face. Be faithful in a little, and He'll give you much. And He'll use you in the little things to prepare you for the greater assignments He has prepared for you. He knows what the assignment will require of you. Great assignments take great character, and the building of character takes time.

DRAWN INTO GOD'S ACTIVITY

I (Mel) was twenty-one years old, driving east across the Mojave Desert in 115-degree weather—in a car with black vinyl interior, no air conditioning, and an engine that was overheating. I was in trouble.

In the distance I saw a dark cloud coming my way. My deliverance! The rain was sure to cool things down, giving much-needed relief. But to my surprise, it wasn't a rainstorm I ran into, but a sandstorm.

Overcome with dust, feeling faint from the scorching temperature, and with a stressed-out car, I searched for a place to stop for help. I was in the middle of nowhere, but eventually I came to a rundown gas station.

The only shade available was the building's shadow, so I pulled around back and parked the car. I got out, opened the hood, and began tinkering with the engine. Suddenly I realized I was being watched. A drifter was standing about thirty feet away, just staring. His hair was unkempt and his face unshaven, and a scar went from his forehead, across his eyelid, and down below his chin. I was nervous. No, I was downright scared!

As the man began to walk straight toward me, many things went through my head. *I'm going to die; nobody will ever find my body; I want my mommy!* Knowing I couldn't run and nobody was there to help, I decided the next best thing was to flash a big smile and hold out my hand to greet a new friend. As we began to talk, he made a fascinating statement: "As I watched you work on your car, you radiated friendliness, and I had to come and meet you."

Immediately I sensed in my spirit what was going on. The Lord was at work, and I needed to respond. As I spoke with the man, I quickly identified what he'd seen in me—the Spirit of God dwelling in my life. As I expected, he was ripe for the picking and responded positively toward Christ.

What had happened? The Father wanted to speak to a desperate man, and He happened to have one of His children driving by. Looking back, I know why my car was overheating, why the storm caused me to stop, and why I ended up behind an old gas station in the backside of the desert. God was at work around me...and the Holy Spirit within me was responding to the orders given by the Father.

IN THE MIDDLE OF GOD'S ACTIVITY

The divine nature cannot be hidden. It must—and it will—express itself. When our lives are yielded to the Spirit's control, God is certain to work through us by leaving His mark on those around us. For not only has He given us new life, He has also extended to us an invitation to be involved in His work to redeem this world. The Holy Spirit's major assignment is to bring our lives into harmony with God's activity so He can accomplish this work through us.

Spiritual gifts don't belong to the believer; rather, they're an expression of the Holy Spirit doing the Father's will. And once you obey God's will for your life, you'll begin to experience the Spirit working through you.

Have you recognized His assignment in *your* life to bring you into the middle of God's activity? One way to begin approaching this is to review your past.

SPIRITUAL MARKERS

Never neglect what you've seen God do in your life. Take a careful look at these things from God's perspective, all the way from your birth to where you stand right now. They're all significant. If you have special talents, use them in the Lord's service. Help another person in need if you have the ability to do so. Step up and bless your church by doing those things that others couldn't do. In other words, be a servant! Don't stand back and watch others struggle when you know you have the ability to lend a hand.

Acts of service, however, are different from the unique assignments God will lay upon your heart. We should always be ready to step up and serve the body of Christ, but what exactly has God called you to invest your life in? What ministries have captured your heart? Is the Lord using your life in such a way that you know the pleasure of God? And what is it that requires the work of the Holy Spirit in order for you to accomplish the task?

In his book *He Shall Glorify Me,* turn-of-the-century preacher Oswald Chambers proclaimed, "The commands of God are enablings. God banks entirely on His own Spirit, and when we attempt, His ability is granted immediately. We have a great deal more power than we know."

As you seek to walk in the center of God's will, it's important to identify the spiritual markers in your life that have led up to where you now stand. Reflect on those moments when you knew God was working and chose to use you. God doesn't work by accident or happenstance; everything He does in your life will lead to the next step in your relationship with Him. Looking back on what God has done in your life may bring great clarity about what He wants to do in your life in the days to come. And as you lay your life before Him, it's amazing how He gives meaning to all that He has built into your life. So bring your past into the present, and ask God to direct your future.

RELATIONSHIP IS THE KEY

Here again we must emphasize this truth: *the relationship is the key.* You must know Christ well enough that you already know your answer before He tells you the assignment. The more you know Him, the more the answer to any assignment will be "Yes, Lord." And if you have a heart of ready obedience, He has a freedom to come to you with any assignment, knowing you'll respond. Your relationship will bring confidence that God knows what He's doing, and it will give you the ability to trust Him.

We must never look first at ourselves, our abilities, and our desires to determine whether we'll obey or not. He is our Lord! If we don't have a heart of obedience, He may choose not to show us His will. For if we knew His will yet still chose not to obey, it would be far better not to have known at all. His mercy withholds the revelation of His will until we're ready to obey. Every time we choose to disobey His clear direction, a hardness comes over our hearts. But when our hearts are prepared to obey, the Holy Spirit has absolute freedom to lead us on in the exciting adventure of following God.

God is always looking upon the heart. So if you're having a hard time hearing from God about His assignment, perhaps He knows your heart isn't ready to respond. That's what God is waiting for—a heart that's surrendered and ready to obey before you ever hear Him speak.

Are you ready for God to reveal His assignment in your life? *Any* assignment? Are you prepared to say yes before you know what He'll ask? That may be the key to knowing and doing the will of God. Your heart must be convinced that He is God and He is Lord.

GOD IS ABLE...AND HE WILL...

I (Henry) have always believed a Christian is primarily called not to a vocation but to a relationship. Our service comes out of our relationship to God through Jesus Christ, and anything He asks, I obey. I still see my life as very ordinary, despite the many areas of ministry in which I've served. How is it that one man has been involved in almost every area of church work, from youth and music to preaching and teaching? How is it that God has taken my life beyond the local church into global mission efforts? How did I become an author and international speaker? Is it because I'm multitalented?

No, it's only because I've sought to be obedient to the Master in all things, and the Holy Spirit has enabled me to serve when God assigns.

Nobody is more surprised at what God is doing through my life than I am. I know my limitations, but I have also come to know the unlimited resources of the Holy Spirit.

Some have asked me if I have a life verse that has guided me. I don't usually use that term, but if I did, the life verse might be a phrase from Daniel 3:17: "Our God whom we serve is able…and He will." The reason I've seen so many miracles in my life is that I've never doubted God's ability to work—and He has.

Assignments and Gifting for the Apostles

Jesus wanted His followers to understand the difference between their best effort and the power of the Holy Spirit. So He sent out seventy disciples two-by-two into the spiritual harvest fields to prepare the way for His own ministry in these areas. As He sent them, He gave them power and authority to fulfill the assignment.

Afterward they could hardly believe what they'd seen God do through their lives. They ministered to people everywhere, healing the sick and proclaiming the kingdom of God. The Scripture says they "returned with joy, saying, 'Lord, even the demons are subject to us in Your name.' And He said to them, 'I saw Satan fall like lightning from heaven. Behold, I give you the authority…'" (Luke 10:17–19).

Jesus let them have a taste of what was to come. This power and authority they experienced was not a permanent gift; it was for *that* assignment. They didn't have natural ability to do what Jesus wanted done, so He gave it to them. As such, they got a foretaste of what was to come with the outpouring of the Holy Spirit on the Day of

Pentecost. They would come to know that anything was possible for God and that if He sent them, He would also equip them.

IN THE OVAL OFFICE

Have you ever had one of those assignments from God that was overwhelming? That seems to be my (Henry) life story. But one particular assignment made me feel especially like a fish out of water.

I was informed that I would be speaking to the president and vice president in the Oval Office. In fact, I was told I could talk with them about anything I wanted. As I prepared, I thought to myself, *What should I say to the president of the United States?* Immediately the Holy Spirit reminded me, *The Father hasn't given you this opportunity so you can tell the president what's on your heart. You're an ambassador of God, to share what's on His heart.* My line of thinking had to be adjusted from self to God. The Holy Spirit was there to enable me to fulfill the Father's purpose.

With God's assignments, it's never about us! The issue is always this: what does *God* want to do with our lives?

Before going into the president's office, I was encouraged to read Luke 12:11–12, "Now when they bring you to the synagogues and magistrates and authorities, do not worry about how or what you should answer, or what you should say. For the Holy Spirit will teach you in that very hour what you ought to say." Indeed, the Spirit gave me the words to say, just as He promised.

NOTHING IS IMPOSSIBLE

There's a moment in Jesus' life when He made a profound statement about the potential in every believer. It's found in the story of a father who brought his demon-possessed son to be healed. Jesus had just come down from the Mount of Transfiguration, when He was met by the desperate father.

This poor man had assumed that the disciples of Jesus had the same power as their Master. But they had been unable to set the son free. You can sense a frustration in Jesus' spirit when he heard of their inability to help this poor child. In fact, this was probably the strongest rebuke He ever gave to the disciples: "O faithless and perverse generation, how long shall I be with you? How long shall I bear with you? Bring him here to Me" (Matthew 17:17).

Once Jesus cast out the demon and cured the boy, the disciples asked a significant question: "Why could we not cast it out?" Jesus summed up His answer with one word—*unbelief.* He went on to contrast their unbelief with the power of true faith: "If you have faith as a mustard seed, you will say to this mountain, 'Move from here to there,' and it will move; and nothing will be impossible for you" (Matthew 17:19–20).

The kind of faith Jesus is looking for is the kind that believes nothing is impossible. That incident for the disciples was critical. They'd been given the power, but unbelief had limited their ability to make a difference in the world.

The same is true with us. Jesus made the promise in John 15:7: "If you abide in Me, and My words abide in you, you will ask what you desire, and it shall be done for you." The questions we must ask are these: Do we believe the Lord? Are we content to live without the promise? Where's the evidence of our belief that God can do the impossible? Especially now that we know the gift of Pentecost, we ought to see the power of God in our lives and in our churches.

THE SPIRIT IS SPEAKING...

What did the Spirit bring to the surface in your life as you read this chapter? Have you been asking the right questions? Or have you never considered that God has a purpose for your life? Did He personalize His constant activity in your life, inviting you to join Him? How have you responded to His activity? Take a moment to pray, along these lines:

Heavenly Father, I see now how deeply You've been working in me all along. Forgive my feeble response, and open my eyes to see and hear You at work. I do want to do Your will, as You make Yourself known to me. May my life be a channel through which You bless those around me. Amen.

CHAPTER 10

KEEPING THE
RELATIONSHIP ALIVE

*Create in me a clean heart, O God, and renew a steadfast
spirit within me. Do not cast me away from Your
presence, and do not take Your Holy Spirit from me.*

—PSALM 51:10–11

My wife and I (Mel) love to ride horses. While on vacation,
we stopped in to visit friends in the Badlands of South
Dakota. They have a huge ranch, and we were going to help them
bring in a herd of cattle that was grazing on government land. On
the way to find the cattle, we had to cross a dry creek bed.

I was riding a big gelding. As I started crossing the creek bed,
the ground began to give way. Before I knew it, I was in quicksand,
and the horse was already down to its belly. Panic hit as I realized
everything underneath me was caving in because of the water still

flowing below the surface. All I knew to do was hold on to the saddle horn, lie across the horse's back, and hold on for dear life.

The horse started fighting to get out. To my amazement, the horse somehow found enough stable earth under the surface to scrape and crawl out of the quicksand. We finally made it back onto solid rock.

Have you ever felt like the ground beneath your life was falling in? What you thought was stable was crumbling, and what you had counted on was no longer there.

FOUNDATIONS IN LIFE

In your life, what's the worst-case scenario that would cause you to sink? What is it that you couldn't live without?

In the Bible, King David recorded his worst-case scenario, and it scared him to death. He felt as though he were in danger of losing something that he simply *must not lose*—and he was terrified.

David cried out to God, "Do not cast me away from Your presence, and do not take Your Holy Spirit from me" (Psalm 51:11). Most people are familiar with the background of this moment in David's life. You know the story: David was in trouble. He had committed grievous sin, terrible sin. The prophet Nathan confronted him, and David realized the evil he had done. He had committed adultery, deceit, and murder. He was guilty. Guilty before God.

David committed these sins after God had chosen him as king...

after God had blessed him with success…and after God had graciously given him far more than he ever deserved. But the greatest gift God had given him was the Holy Spirit.

David knew there would be consequences for his sin; he knew life would never be the same. So he cried out, "God, I'm guilty! God, have mercy on me! I know there are consequences. But God, whatever You do, don't take Your Spirit from me!"

It was the cry of a man on the edge of the abyss; it came from a man who suddenly felt as though the foundations of his world were caving in: "Don't cast me from Your presence, and don't take Your Spirit from me!"

So often when we hear that phrase, "Don't take Your Spirit from me," we tune out. We feel David's pain, but we conclude, "That doesn't apply to me. I haven't done such grievous sin; I haven't come to that point of rebellion in my life."

Or we rationalize theologically: "That was before Jesus paid the price for sin on the cross, before His death and resurrection, and before Pentecost and the coming of the Spirit. Now things are different; God doesn't take His Spirit away from those who have been born again. So I'm safe."

But think about this for a moment: Have you ever been in a place where your faith has become weak, shaky, and in danger of failing? Have you known moments when the pressure of life, with all its frustrations, threatened to extinguish the flame that once burned bright?

Suppose the flame of your inner spirit begins to flicker and you feel it may soon be extinguished. Maybe at some point you've cried out like this: "Lord, I'm struggling, and I feel like I'm losing my relationship with You. My spirit is dry, and I don't know what to do. What's going on, Lord? *Take not Your Spirit from me.*"

You may not be in danger of losing your salvation, but are you in danger of losing the intimate relationship to God that's the foundation of your life? What does it mean to possess and lose the relationship?

TO HAVE OR TO LOSE

To understand what it means to lose the relationship with the Spirit, you must understand fully what it feels like to have it.

To be spiritually alive is…

- to *be aware of and obedient to* the Spirit's inner voice that speaks to your heart
- to have *faith* that takes God at His word
- to have a *hope* that looks beyond the darkness to the coming dawn
- to have a *love* that sees in every person a brother or sister for whom Christ died
- to be *alive* to the existence of an unseen spiritual world that is real
- to *live* for the eternal and *seek first* the kingdom of God

That's what it looks like to live in the Spirit. That's what it means to be alive in Christ and functioning in good health within the family of God

Resisting the work of God's Spirit has devastating effects upon your life that are obvious to all. To be spiritually dead is...

- to be *unresponsive* to the Spirit's still, small voice and *insensitive* to the living God
- to grow *skeptical* about faith, *disillusioned* about hope, *cynical* about love
- to feel that the struggle between good and evil is *not worth the battle*
- to find your spiritual zeal *smothered* by the dreariness of life
- to *lose the excitement* of walking by faith and attempting the impossible
- to *stop caring* about the body of Christ, the people of God, and be *apathetic* toward the church
- to be *insensitive* to the millions of souls headed toward eternity without a hope of finding heaven
- to find prayer *useless* and *not worth the effort*

Those statements describe what it looks like to lose the Spirit's work in your life. Any one of them ought to make you tremble!

Our hearts cry out, "Dear God, don't let my heart drift from Your presence. *Take not Thy Spirit from me.*" But can it happen? Does God remove His Spirit? Would He ever really do such a thing?

We think of the Bible verses where God says, "I will never leave you nor forsake you" (Hebrews 13:5), or "Lo, I am with you always, even to the end of the age" (Matthew 28:20). Surely God wouldn't take His Spirit away from us!

Would God ever say, "I'm done with that guy! I'm leaving him to fend for himself!" Does He ever remove His Spirit? That question has been greatly debated. Some believe He will; others say He won't.

Biblically, once a person has truly been born again, that person remains a child of God. But that speaks more to the issue of salvation. What about the work of the Spirit in our lives? Undoubtedly there are things that can break our fellowship with God—things that create a barrier and disqualify us for the intimate work of the Spirit.

Sometimes our problem is simply neglect. Neglect of anything leads to atrophy and decay. If we don't use our capacity to respond to the Spirit and choose to walk by faith, the ability fades.

Neglect is a passive thing, which is why it's so easy to fall into. We don't actively look for God; we don't actively listen for Him. We just get busy living our lives and fail to give God the attention due Him.

But we can also lose the relationship through rebellion. Allowing sin to cover our souls will always keep us from responding positively to the Holy Spirit. That's what David did: he chose to disobey God when he followed his own desires and disregarded God's law. His later realization of what he had done caused him to write Psalm 51.

In our lives, when we refuse to listen to the prompting of God's Spirit, we become callous to His voice, creating a barrier that hardens our hearts. When this happened to David, he finally realized that his relationship with God was slipping. That's why he cried out, "Take not Your Spirit from me. Create in me a clean heart, O God, a heart that is tender toward You." David realized he could afford to lose many things, but *not the Spirit.* He knew that if the Spirit left, there would be no light to guide, no voice to interpret, no hand to steady or control. If he lost the Spirit, his life wasn't worth living. He was terrified of losing the Spirit.

But once we get to this point—a point of desperation in wanting the presence of God's Spirit—we're in a good place. The fact that David cried out is evidence that the Spirit *was still there.* So let's consider how we ought to respond when the Holy Spirit begins to move in our lives.

OUR RESPONSE TO THE GIFT

How we receive the gift of the Holy Spirit will determine the course of our lives. Our response to the Spirit is the reason we either see Him working in power or are frustrated in our walk with Christ. It's the determining factor in whether we'll experience the blessing of the Lord or His discipline.

The Holy Spirit desires full and complete control of our lives. Every ounce of our being must be fully surrendered to Him so He can fully do the Father's will through us. If the smallest part of our lives is not yielded to Him, it can derail His work to accomplish the Father's

Only in Acts
+ once in
Eph 5.

will. This may be why the Bible speaks of being filled with the Spirit and of the baptism of the Holy Spirit (meaning "total immersion in the Spirit") in order to impress upon us that He must have complete control of our lives.

When we fully realize that God, through His Spirit, is actively at work in our lives, we ought to respond with holy awe. There ought to come over us a trembling fear that we might upset the Holy Spirit. As Paul said, "Work out your own salvation with fear and trembling; for it is God who works in you both to will and to do for His good pleasure" (Philippians 2:12–13).

Let's take a look at different responses to the Holy Spirit among people today.

GRIEVING THE SPIRIT

First, we can *grieve* the Holy Spirit: "And do not grieve the Holy Sprit of God, by whom you were sealed for the day of redemption. Let all bitterness, wrath, anger, clamor, and evil speaking be put away from you, with all malice" (Ephesians 4:30–31).

Simply put, sin in our lives grieves the Holy Spirit. When we allow attitudes and actions to be controlled by the flesh instead of the Spirit, we offend the Spirit within us. When those actions cause a break in fellowship with another believer, it also causes a break in fellowship with Him.

The Spirit cannot lead us into God's blessing until we repent of our sin, so He immediately brings conviction of the truth and the strength to repent.

Never forget that the Spirit's work of confronting us with our sin is done from a deep sense of love. The initial response of the Holy Spirit to our sin is not anger, but grief. Our sin grieves Him, for He knows how it will rob us of God's best and rob others of God's best through us.

RESISTING THE SPIRIT

Second, we can *resist* the Holy Spirit. Stephen told the people, "You stiff-necked and uncircumcised in heart and ears! You always resist the Holy Spirit; as your fathers did, so do you" (Acts 7:51).

When our sin grieves the Holy Spirit, He immediately brings conviction. But when He comes to bring our sin to light, urging us to repent, we can resist Him. We can refuse to admit our sin or soft-pedal its name so it doesn't sound so bad. We call adultery an "affair," homosexuality an "alternate lifestyle," the murder of unborn babies "pro-choice." We excuse our anger by blaming our past, we justify our unforgiveness, and we refuse to heed the work of the Holy Spirit in our lives. We resist His work to make us holy and acceptable to God and become disqualified for service.

Perhaps the most common form of resistance is found in simple complacency. We aren't alert and looking for the Spirit's activity. We want His presence only when we call Him in to meet our needs. We resist Him in worship during the invitation when He brings conviction. We postpone the encounter for another time, never realizing we're putting off God when we resist His Spirit. Or when He speaks, we argue, offer another opinion, or tune Him out. But when He speaks, the issue isn't open for discussion; He's looking for immediate obedience.

Noted theologian and author Andrew Murray wrote in his book *In Search of Spiritual Excellence:*

> My brethren, it is an unspeakable holy and glorious thing that a man can be filled with the Spirit of God. It demands inevitably that the present occupant and governor of the heart, our individual self, be cast out and everything be surrendered into the hands of the new inhabitant, the Spirit of God. If only we could understand that the joy and power of being filled with the Spirit will come once we comply with the first and principal condition—namely, that He alone be acknowledged as our Life and our Leader.

Another of the reasons we resist the work of the Holy Spirit is that He'll often speak through another person. We may not mind if He speaks to our hearts while we are alone with Him, but when He does it through a brother or sister in the Lord, we resist Him. A penetrating word in a sermon, a comment made by another person in our Bible study group, or the private counsel of a friend can assault our pride, and we struggle. But Jesus said, "He who receives whomever I send receives Me; and he who receives Me receives Him who sent Me" (John 13:20). If we refuse to hear a corrective word from another Christian and thereby separate ourselves from the life of God's people, we're not in a position to hear the Spirit. He works through other Christians, and we resist Him by not allowing them into our lives.

QUENCHING THE SPIRIT

A third response is to *quench* the Spirit. Paul said, "Do not quench the Spirit. Do not despise prophecies. Test all things; hold fast what is good. Abstain from every form of evil" (1 Thessalonians 5:19–22). In this context, the quenching appears to involve hindering or stifling the Spirit in some way. When the fire of the Spirit is burning, someone pours water on it or turns a meeting away from the Lord by a selfish or carnal comment.

We often pray for revival or for a great movement of the Spirit, yet we're unreceptive when He comes. We want conviction among the lost, but He instead calls believers to repentance. We envision how the church will be blessed, but He takes the church in a direction we aren't comfortable with. Because the Spirit doesn't come as we want, we turn Him away. But if the Holy Spirit is truly God, we don't tell Him how to work in our lives. He comes with the right to do as He pleases.

All three of these negative attitudes—grieving, resisting, and quenching—will keep the Holy Spirit from working in and through our lives. Sadly, they're common in the church today. People don't want the Spirit of Truth to reveal the truth about their lives. We even use Christian activity as a cloak to hide the truth from ourselves and others.

THERE ARE CONSEQUENCES

I (Henry) was once approached by a man who confessed to me a tragic and disturbing testimony. Two years earlier, when he was a pastor in a large church, he'd become involved in an improper relationship with his secretary. He'd chosen to divorce his wife and marry the woman, shattering relationships with his family and friends. Now he was trying to get on with his life and find a place of ministry within the pastorate again. He looked to me and asked, "Would you pray for me?"

My response wasn't what he was expecting. In fact, he probably wanted to retract the request. I said, "Yes, I will pray for you, but you need to know how I'll pray. I will pray that God deals with you in such a way that anyone even thinking of doing what you've done will forever be deterred from such a grievous sin." That man had no idea what it meant to openly sin against God and the convicting work of the Holy Spirit. There are consequences!

One needs only to read Hebrews 10:26–29:

For if we sin willfully after we have received the knowledge of the truth, there no longer remains a sacrifice for sins, but a certain fearful expectation of judgment, and fiery indignation which will devour the adversaries. Anyone who has rejected Moses' law dies without mercy on the testimony of two or three witnesses. Of how much worse punishment, do you suppose, will he be thought worthy who has trampled the Son of God underfoot, counted the blood of the covenant by which he was sanctified a common thing, and insulted the Spirit of grace?

ASSIGNMENT DEPENDS ON CHARACTER

We live in a generation that feels as though there should be no consequences to our sin—including no restrictions on our "spiritual gifts." We say to ourselves, "After all, God is love and He'll forgive, won't He? Can't I continue to serve according to my gifts?"

It's true He forgives the repentant sinner, but that isn't the issue. The assignments of God always depend on character, not gifts. He'll bypass thousands of people with impressive gifts to find one person whose heart is pure.

Hudson Taylor, pioneer missionary to China, once said:

God gives His Holy Spirit not to those who long for Him,
not to those who pray for Him, not to those who desire to
always be filled. He gives His Spirit to those who obey.

Again, the building of such character takes time. This is why it's
important to respond when the Holy Spirit is working in your life.
If you consistently resist the convicting work of the Spirit—who's
trying to keep you from sin—you've just revealed a deep character
flaw.

Remember, serving God is a privilege, not a right. Never tell
God what you think you ought to do; He doesn't care about that.
He wants to work through you, but He chooses not to work through
an unholy vessel who will not yield to His Spirit.

FILLED WITH THE SPIRIT

The good news is that we're free in Christ not to quench or resist or
grieve the Spirit. Every person has the ability, by creation, to walk in
an intimate relationship with the holy God by being filled with the
Spirit. Paul said, "Do not be drunk with wine, in which is dissipation;
but be filled with the Spirit" (Ephesians 5:18). When we respond to
His work and yield to His right to reign in us, He then fills us.

It's helpful to think of this filling in the context of the other
three attitudes, for if we don't, we'll think of being filled with the
Spirit as merely an additional blessing or an extra inheritance that

other Christians don't have. It will cause us to strive after something beyond our grasp, and this will cause much frustration.

The truth is this: if we aren't filled with the Spirit at any given moment, it's because of only one thing—sin. Through sin, we grieve the Spirit, resist Him, and quench His work in our lives. When our lives are clean, when we're walking in a right relationship with the Lord, the Holy Spirit has complete access to our lives.

From God's perspective, being filled with the Spirit is the normal Christian life, which is what He desires for each of His children. And the place of filling is at the cross, where Jesus forgives our sin and covers us with His righteousness. As we allow Him to remove our sin, He fills us with the Spirit.

The formula for living the Spirit-filled life is simple: *obedience.* We have no need of the Holy Spirit if we aren't willing to do what God has asked of us. The power of the Spirit will be seen at our first step of obedience.

THE SPIRIT IS SPEAKING...

Has the Holy Spirit convicted you of any sin in your life, even while you've been reading this book? Do not grieve Him any longer. Repent and turn from your sin and take hold of the promises of God. Allow the Holy Spirit to fill your life so you can experience abundant life in Christ.

The moment King David cried out in repentance, he was nearer the heart of God than he'd been in a long time. It can be the same for you.

Have you failed the Lord? Do you realize you're not where you used to be? Do you know your heart is not as tender as it once was? Have you lost the zeal for the Lord you once had? Do you no longer find joy in serving Him? Do you no longer love the people of God? Are you apathetic toward the lost people all around you? Do you hesitate to walk by faith or refuse to sacrifice anything for the Lord? Have you stopped seeking first the kingdom and pursued other goals in life?

If that's you...*does it bother you?* Are you restless because you know you're not experiencing what God intended when He gave you the gift of His Spirit? If so, you're in a good place today! The Spirit is speaking to your heart.

Every person has the opportunity to establish or renew an intimate relationship with God through the work of His Spirit. When you stop everything and cry out, "Lord, forgive my sin and fill me with Your Spirit!"—He hears. He will hear when you cry out, "Don't let me act according to the flesh, but by Your Spirit. Don't let me serve according to my ability, but by Your Spirit. Don't let me reason out the decisions in my life, but teach me to respond to Your Spirit. Don't let me see life through my eyes alone, but may Your Spirit open my eyes to see *You.* Lord, create in me a clean heart, and restore the joy of Your salvation!"

Take a moment to pray along these lines:

"Heavenly Father, I don't want to miss out on Your best. If I've been grieving, resisting, or quenching the blessed work of Your Spirit in my life, then this is to my shame and Your dishonor. May Your Holy Spirit search my heart to see if there be any wicked way in me. Forgive me, cleanse me, and use me as You will. Amen."

In your prayer, you may want to name specific areas of your life you've been withholding from Him. Repentance must be specific.

Chapter II

A LIFE FILLED TO THE FULL

Most assuredly, I say to you, he who believes in Me, the works that I do he will do also; and greater works than these he will do, because I go to My Father.

—John 14:12

When we allow Christ to function as Lord of our lives and the Spirit is free to actively work in us, the difference will become obvious. Life no longer consists of merely doing good works for God. Instead, the Christian life proves to be an exciting adventure of walking in God's very presence.

Eternal life is not going to heaven when you die. It's a living relationship with God that begins at salvation and extends into eternity.

TAKING THE PLUNGE

In my (Mel) college days, I went with friends to explore the beautiful Lynn Valley Canyon in North Vancouver. In the valley was a fast-flowing river fed by snowmelt coming off the mountains. At one point, the narrow river briefly widened into a pool with a steep rock wall towering over it. As we approached, the girls gasped at the bravery of some men jumping off the cliffs. "They have no fear! I can't believe anyone would do that! They're so brave!" Well, as you can imagine, I was cool—willing to do whatever necessary to impress my friends. Before I had time to think about what came out of my mouth, I confidently announced, "I could do that!"

Immediately I realized that talk is cheap. Anyone can boast about things they haven't yet done. As I climbed up the "cliff of death," the people below looked smaller and the boulders beneath the crystal-clear water appeared larger. I remember thinking, *Why did I open my big mouth?* There I stood at the edge of the cliff with nothing between me and a fifty-foot drop into ice-cold water. All I needed was the courage to do it.

I took one simple step, and there was no turning back. The wind came rushing through my hair, and the adrenaline was surging. Fear turned to excitement. I plunged deep into the pool.

As I shot out of the water to a crowd of cheering onlookers, my first thought was, *I'm alive!* Second thought: *Let's do it again!*

THE LOOK OF ADVENTURE

Many believers are unwilling to take a step of faith and release their lives into the Spirit's control. They remain comfortable within their range of talents and hesitate to attempt anything beyond. But what an adventure it is to walk in the Spirit!

What does that adventure look like? What can you expect to experience when you choose to walk in the Spirit?

To again quote A. J. Gordon, it will mean "this difference, that whereas before, it was hard for us to do the easiest things, now it is easy for us to do the hard things."

As you continue in this journey, you'll notice several distinctive characteristics of a person who has understood the Christian life and is walking in the Spirit.

SATISFACTION WITH CHRIST

First, there's *satisfaction with Christ.* This may sound simple, but it's absolutely necessary if we're to be of use to God. We must be satisfied in Him, or we'll be constantly thinking of ourselves and our personal needs.

Jesus said, "Whoever drinks of the water that I shall give him will never thirst. But the water that I shall give him will become in him a fountain of water springing up into everlasting life" (John 4:14). A relationship with Christ satisfies, and the Holy Spirit is the key. Jesus also said, "If anyone thirsts, let him come to Me and drink. He who believes in Me, as the Scripture has said, out of his heart will flow rivers of living water." He satisfies! John told us that Jesus was speaking of "the Spirit, whom those believing in Him would receive" (John 7:37–39). The Spirit is the one who applies to our lives all that Christ accomplished on our behalf.

Once you recognize your need, Jesus says, "Come to Me and drink." Come not to anyone else—not to a church, a ministry, or a noble cause—but "come to *Me*."

He gave His life that you might be filled. He laid aside His glory that you might be filled. He prayed that you might be filled. He ascended on high, sits on the throne, has all authority in heaven and on earth, and sent His Holy Spirit that you might be filled. He has prepared everything necessary to fill your life with rivers of living water that will refresh your soul, and He now extends the invitation: "Come and drink." And when we do, we're satisfied.

DISSATISFACTION WITH SELF

Satisfaction with Christ leads to *dissatisfaction with self*, another distinctive mark of those who walk in the Spirit. You'll discover that the Holy Spirit will always be urging you to put aside anything that will hinder your progress as you run the race set before you.

When we seek the Spirit, He'll always seek to make us holy and acceptable to God (see Romans 12:1). Someone who's born again of the Spirit will be putting off sin and putting on righteousness (see Ephesians 4:17–24; Colossians 3:1–13).

You can easily spot a person who has come near the kingdom of God and is under the conviction of the Holy Spirit. That person's mouth is stopped—no more excuses, no more explaining away sinful behavior. He or she humbly kneels at the cross and says, "God, forgive me, a sinner." This person is growing daily toward Christlikeness.

HUNGER TO KNOW CHRIST MORE

That leads to the next characteristic, a *hunger to know Christ more.* The words in the Bible about Christ are no longer hearsay, rather He's real and personal in *your* life. The Spirit continually uncovers the riches of Christ, and you see Him as never before. As your mind is occupied by thoughts of Christ, He occupies your life and actions as well, so that Christ is revealed in an ever-increasing measure.

Then we can say, as Paul did to the Christians in Philippi, "For to me, to live is Christ" (Philippians 1:21). And notice the intensity in Paul's voice as he later told them, "I also count all things loss for the excellence of the knowledge of Christ Jesus my Lord…that I may know Him and the power of His resurrection, and the fellowship of His sufferings, being conformed to His death" (Philippians 3:8, 10).

LOVE FOR GOD'S PEOPLE

Another characteristic of believers walking in the Spirit—one that's especially obvious—is that they *love the people of God.* They always seek to build up the body of Christ and are willing to lay down their lives for them. The Spirit is given not for the individual alone but to strengthen and build up the church (see Ephesians 4:7, 11–16).

One of the clearest evidences of a Spirit-filled life is a person's interdependent relationship with the rest of God's people. He or she loves the family of God and is using Spirit-given gifts to strengthen and build them up. Paul said, "We, being many, are one body in Christ, and individually members of one another" (Romans 12:5). It's never a matter of finding your spiritual gifts and going off to do your ministry alone or outside the context of the church. Any equipping of the Spirit is to help bring every member to complete Christlikeness.

People who are filled with the Spirit cannot stand outside the church and watch from a distance. It's spiritually impossible! They realize every Christian is a brother or sister in Christ. And in Christ, we're *blood relatives*. The words of John say it all: "By this we know love, because He laid down His life for us. And we also ought to lay down our lives for the brethren" (1 John 3:16).

Walking with Christ and being filled with the Spirit is what God desires for all His children to experience. It's practical; it's life in the real world.

Listen to a few simple stories that demonstrate what this life looks like.

Have My Cake and Eat It Too

The greatest joy of being a pastor is to teach people truth and then see them apply it in their lives. In fact, nothing brings a smile to my (Mel) face more than watching God work in and through people's lives.

Tonya is the wife of a staff member, and she has learned to walk in the Spirit. She's constantly listening to the Spirit guide her life. But you need to know a little about Tonya. Some people are very organized in their shopping, efficiently going through their grocery lists and stocking up for the week. Not Tonya. She refers to herself as a pinball shopper. She bounces around from here to there, often making many trips back to the store for things she forgot. And since she's very sociable, the benefit to this shopping technique is that she gets to greet a lot of people.

One day she came through the checkout line and didn't recognize the woman at the register. That was odd, for Tonya knew everybody who worked there. She later learned that this woman, Carla, had recently moved to the area and was struggling to make ends meet. She was currently in a relationship with a man, and both had children from a previous marriage. There were a lot of children involved, and it was a challenge to keep them all clothed, fed, and cared for on a limited budget. As Tonya began a "grocery store friendship" with her, she also quickly discovered that Carla had been very hurt by churches and was wounded very deeply.

Not long after they met, Tonya was planning a trip to the store to pick up a birthday cake. In fact, it was *her* birthday. She'd ordered her favorite cake and was looking forward to celebrating the day with her husband and three children. Before she picked up the cake, however, the Spirit of God began to speak to her: "Tonya, I want you to give your birthday cake to Carla." It sounded odd, but at the same time the message was clear.

The day was very busy, and Tonya hadn't had time to get to the store. But the Lord wouldn't let her forget, as the Spirit constantly reminded her of what He said. So she made time to go to the store for that one item.

Her timing was perfect: Carla was in the express checkout line, and there weren't many people around. Tonya got the cake and came through the line. After paying, Tonya said to Carla, "Today's my birthday, and the Lord has asked me to give this to you so you can celebrate with your family. I know extras are hard to come by."

Carla immediately broke into tears, and she became embarrassed as other customers approached her register. Tonya slipped away with the assurance that she'd obeyed the Lord.

The next day, we received a phone call at our church. The caller asked about a lady named Tonya. The call was from Carla's mother, who had been praying for her daughter who had wandered away from God. She'd heard the story of what Tonya did and how overwhelmed Carla was by the kindness she was shown. This poor mother had been praying for her daughter for years. Now she could not stop talking about the impact Tonya had made upon her prodigal child. For the first time in a long time, Carla wanted to go back to church.

Tonya's responsiveness to the Holy Spirit set off a chain of events that would impact a family for eternity. Carla's family started coming to the church. The church had the opportunity to meet other needs in their home. A few months later, the couple was married, joined the church, and began to grow in the Lord.

Where did it all start? It began in the heart of God. Then the Holy Spirit took the will of God and impressed it upon one of His children. Fortunately, Tonya had learned to recognize the voice of God and respond in obedience. And because she was willing to respond in obedience—even when it didn't make sense—a family was transformed.

MISSING YOU

Frank is one of the kindest and most gracious men I (Mel) know. He served the Lord as a pastor for many years before he taught in a Christian university. By the time I knew him, he was of retirement age and was teaching in a seminary as a visiting professor. While there, he joined our church and became involved in Sunday school.

One particular day, as Frank was getting his car washed, the Holy Spirit told him to go by the car dealership and see the mechanic. The mechanic was a man named John who had visited our church a few times and had actually gone twice to Frank's Sunday school class, but he hadn't been back since.

John was a man's man. He was very big and athletic, and he enjoyed his intimidating appearance. Frank, on the other hand, had a slight build, white hair, and fair skin. He was a suit-and-tie kind of guy, and John's world of auto mechanics was somewhat foreign to him. They had nothing in common.

The Holy Spirit, however, laid a burden on Frank's heart to go see John. It sounded strange, and Frank admitted he didn't really want to go. In fact, when he finished with the car wash, he turned to drive home. But immediately the Holy Spirit said, "You're going the wrong way. Turn around and go to the car dealership."

Frank turned around. At the dealership, he went to the front desk and asked if he could speak to John. After a few minutes, the mechanic, wearing blue overalls and covered in grease, emerged from the garage with a bewildered look on his face. Frank, wearing a suit with a white shirt and tie, approached John with a big smile and gave him a hug. Then he said, "I just want you to know I've missed you at church the past few weeks. We love you and want you to come back." Then he left.

In that moment, the Spirit of God penetrated John's heart. That encounter broke down every barrier and was the turning point in his life. John had struggled with sin for years and felt riddled with guilt.

When he'd reached out to churches in the past, he had been met with condemnation. As a result, he resigned himself to the fact that he could never know God.

As I talked with John later, he described the encounter with Frank like this: "I know Frank is a godly man; you can just see it on his face. I know I'm not walking with God, but I believe God speaks to Frank. And when God told him to come see me, I realized God must love me." Tears began to stream down his face as he continued: "When Frank came and gave me a hug, it was as if God Himself had wrapped His arms around me and I was loved. In that moment, He set me free."

GOD IS CALLING

A young lady named Roni had been invited to our church. Her story was complicated. She was a divorced single mom struggling to raise two teenage girls who were rebelling. Life seemed to be falling apart, but she couldn't bring herself to trust God. She'd reluctantly come to the church on occasion, but she kept her distance. It was all so foreign.

But something inside was drawing her to find out more. So she attended a Bible study designed to introduce non-Christians to the Christian faith. Susan was leading the group and tried to build a relationship with her. But Roni refused to let her get too close and backed away, eventually dropping out of the Bible study.

One morning, however, she was up at five getting ready for a business trip. While in the shower, she remembered a sermon that I (Mel) preached on prayer. She'd never prayed before but decided to give it a try. The essence of her prayer was simple: "God, if You're really there, I need for You to make Yourself known."

At that exact moment, the phone rang. A little startled by the phone ringing at five in the morning, she hesitated to answer. By the time she got to the phone, it had stopped ringing. As she continued getting ready, the phone rang again. She wondered, *Who in the world is calling me at this hour?*

She answered the phone. It was Susan. "Roni, I'm so sorry for calling you this early. But God woke me up and told me to call you. He wants you to know He loves you."

Roni was stunned. She could hardly believe that God was conveying to her a message of His love…by awakening Susan to call her…right after she prayed…at five o'clock in the morning. As a result, Roni eventually gave her life to Christ, was baptized, and married a Christian man. Her life would never be the same again.

Later I told Susan, "I can't believe you called Roni so early. Why didn't you wait until a decent hour?"

"I've never done that before," she answered. "I couldn't believe I was calling her. But the Holy Spirit clearly led me, and I had to obey." Then she added, "I felt so foolish, but what would have happened if I hadn't obeyed?"

THE SPIRIT IS SPEAKING...

Since your first step of faith that brought salvation, have you continued growing in your relationship to Christ through the Holy Spirit? Have you learned to recognize the prompting of the Spirit?

Do you realize the Holy Spirit can open up whole new opportunities for your life, if only you learn to listen and obey?

Don't limit your life by human reasoning, but trust your relationship to Him. There's so much more to know and experience personally of God, so keep moving forward and allow Him to take you into the sphere of His activity.

Take a moment and ask God to keep your heart focused on Him and His activity. And when the Spirit speaks, make the adjustments to obey, no matter how foolish it may seem.

He knows what He's doing. And He's the key to abundant life.

CHAPTER 12

COMPLETE SURRENDER

*For whoever desires to save his life will lose it, but
whoever loses his life for My sake will find it.*

—MATTHEW 16:25

The key to a growing relationship with God is to release your
life to all you know. Don't worry about the unknown; simply
respond to what He has revealed. If you're faithful in a little, He'll
give you more. Don't just look toward some future time when He'll
do great things in your life; each step along the journey is special.
And each step will open up new opportunities.

You'll discover that the power of the Holy Spirit is profoundly
simple. You'll also find that your relationship to God is uniquely
your own. He'll take you from where you are to where He wants you
to be. At the beginning of the journey, you won't know all the details or where He's taking you, but you can trust that His will is
always best.

YIELDING TO THE SPIRIT'S WORK

You may have given your life to Christ, but have you understood that you must yield your life to the work of the Holy Spirit? There's no such thing as a once-for-all decision in the Christian life; it's a daily dying to self—daily seeking Him and bowing to His lordship. That Spirit-led lifestyle must start somewhere; have you made the deliberate decision to allow the Holy Spirit to have complete access to your life?

That question can be answered more easily by asking it another way: do you make your decisions based upon your ability to achieve the results or upon the Spirit's leading and equipping?

Don't determine your response to God by looking at your gifts. Look at your Lord and say, "Yes, Lord! I know Your Spirit is present to enable me as I obey You. Thank You, Lord!"

THE ISSUE SETTLED

Many people have asked about the moment when I (Henry) fully surrendered my life to the Lord. That moment occurred at the age of nine when I was confronted with a simple truth: God convinced me that He was God and I was not. It may sound simple, but that special encounter has shaped my life ever since, and I've never approached God any other way.

It wasn't until my teen years that I began to understand the implications of this truth. At the age of seventeen, I was at a youth rally filled with people, but it seemed as though I was the only person in the room. God came to me and said, *I told you that I am God and have the right to your life. I'm claiming that right tonight.*

In that call of God, everything came into focus as I understood what it meant to surrender my life. In that moment I settled the issue of Christ's lordship, and I've never turned back. I released my life as much as I knew how as a teenage boy, knowing I would need the Holy Spirit to guide me. I set my heart to obey and have never had to go back through the process again. It was settled.

If Jesus is Lord, there's no need to wrestle with the decision to obey. I just need to know what He wants of my life, I've discovered over time that my response to each assignment determines what He'll do next. And He has been everything He ever said He would be in my life.

Releasing Control

I (Mel) also became a Christian at age nine. It was a childlike faith, because that's all a child has! As I grew in my knowledge of the Lord, I realized God's call on my life. But not until a few years later did I understand what that meant.

I was still trying to do God's will in my own strength and failing miserably. I was very active in church, a leader among my peers, and doing what I thought was best—but with no power. It was becoming obvious I had no idea what to do; it was clear I was wasting time and missing God's purposes.

Thank God He got my attention! It happened through an accident I had on a temporary logging job in northern Canada. As I lay in the snow—my femur shattered, my chainsaw still buzzing, and the temperature at thirty-five degrees below zero—the Lord said, *If you're not going to be of any use to Me on earth, you have no reason to be here. I could take you home at any time.*

In that moment I knew I had to give Him my entire life. It wasn't what I could do for God; it was what He wanted to do through me. And until that moment I had been scared to release control to Him. I finally realized my body didn't belong to me; it was His to use as He wanted.

My life hasn't been the same since. That doesn't mean I've been coasting on cloud nine with miracles left and right. But the Spirit has consistently taught me, shaped me, and used me for the Father's purpose. Each act of obedience has opened up new opportunities to serve Him.

SEEING THE SCARS

Anyone who yields his or her life to God will be greatly used by God to extend His kingdom. The nature of God's great salvation is that not only are you brought into the family of God, but you're also given the privilege of being a part of His plan to redeem the world. He comes to every believer with the invitation to respond to His work in and around that person's life.

Does that get you excited? It ought to, for there's no higher calling in life than to have the God of the universe invite you to join Him. So stand ready to respond!

After Jesus was resurrected, a fascinating event occurred in the room when He appeared to the gathered disciples. He showed them the wounds on His hands and His side, as if to say, "Here's My identification. *I am Jesus!*" What a picture of love! Then He said to the disciples, "Peace to you! As the Father has sent Me, I also send you" (John 20:21).

This passage doesn't say what the disciples were thinking at this moment of their commissioning, but they must have been staring at those scars—scars that reminded them that there was a cost, there was pain, there was a cross for them to bear as well. For Jesus had just stated that they were being sent *just as the Father had sent Jesus,* to do the Father's will.

Oswald Chambers wrote in *My Utmost for His Highest:*

Every element of our own self-reliance must be put to death by the power of God. The moment we recognize our complete weakness and our dependence upon Him will be the very moment that the Spirit of God will exhibit His power.

Remember again that when Jesus was sent by the Father, He was equipped with the Holy Spirit. In the same way, the disciples would be equipped with power from on high. Listen to the record of John immediately after this assignment was given to the disciples: "And when He had said this, He breathed on them, and said to them, 'Receive the Holy Spirit'" (John 20:22). Here was the enabling work of the Holy Spirit coming upon them.

Soon afterward, Pentecost was the moment when the Spirit was sent upon all believers in a permanent fashion. He came upon them to be Jesus in them, and much more. In the same way Jesus had taught, now the Spirit would teach. As Jesus had comforted, now the Spirit would comfort. As Jesus had led, now the Spirit would lead. Everything they would need would be found in Him who now dwelt within. And their mission would be the proclamation of the gospel of salvation throughout the world.

GOD WILL SHOW YOU

Listen to God's wonderful promise:

> Thus says the LORD who made it, the LORD who formed it
> to establish it (the LORD is His name): "Call to Me, and I
> will answer you, and show you great and mighty things,
> which you do not know. (Jeremiah 33:2–3)

Are there things about God's will you don't know? Then be ready for God to reveal His purposes through the Holy Spirit who dwells within you. Don't be in a hurry; simply trust that He'll show you in His time what's on His heart. He may cause you to wait before Him. He may choose to leave you in a difficult situation to see whether you'll remain faithful. He's far more concerned with who you are than with what you do for Him. So go to Him with an open Bible, and ask Him to reveal His purposes for your life, purposes that were established before you were ever created.

The Bible teaches that nobody can thwart God's plans for you (Romans 8:31). Satan can't stop you, the world can't stop you, and circumstances can't stop you. "If God is for us, who can be against us?" (Romans 8:31).

COUNTING THE COST

I (Henry) was leading a conference in Taiwan when scores of people began responding to the message on revival. Before I finished speaking, people began streaming forward.

When appropriate, I came alongside a young man who was kneeling at the front, for it was obvious the Holy Spirit was dealing with him. His eyes were swollen with tears, and he was visibly shaking.

I said to him, "It seems to me that God has spoken to you."

He quietly answered, "Yes sir."

"Do you mind telling me what He said?"

He looked directly into my eyes. "God has told me I'm to go to mainland China and preach the gospel."

I asked if he realized this could cost him his life.

As he looked back at me, it seemed as though I could see right into his soul. After a moment he said through tears, "Sir—that's the issue I just settled with God a few minutes ago."

That young man had a profound encounter with God, and the Holy Spirit was guiding him in understanding it. The Lord was leading him to a new level of obedience that would be costly. But he surrendered his life to be used of God no matter what the cost.

Like Abraham climbing the mountain with Isaac to make the ultimate sacrifice, this man had a faith that was ready to say yes to anything God asked. And in the midst of tears, there was great joy that the Lord counted him worthy of such an assignment. But he didn't go alone; he went full of the Holy Spirit. His confidence wasn't in self, but in the Spirit's ability to work through his life to accomplish the Lord's will.

GOD IS WHERE YOU ARE NOT

My wife and I (Henry) have traveled to around 110 countries of the world, often for the purpose of strengthening and encouraging our missionaries. We've discovered that one of the greatest deterrents for people going to the foreign mission field is the pressure of parents. Many parents don't want a child to move away from them, especially if there are grandchildren involved. But they don't realize that the greatest single honor that parents can have is for the God of the universe to choose one of their own. Parents need to release their children to follow the Lord, wherever that might be.

Another difficult dimension to following the Lord was evident one time when we were speaking to a group of missionaries in East Africa. One of the men who had served there for ten years stood up. "I need prayer," he said. "I'm struggling with the fact that I'm over here in Africa sharing the gospel with those who are lost, and my mom and dad back home are getting older, and they don't know Christ. I'm struggling to know whether I should stay here or go home and seek to lead them to Christ."

We came around him to pray, and we wept with him on behalf of his parents.

Not long after that, we were back at home when we received a report about the parents of this dear missionary. They had experienced a sudden desire to visit a nearby country church. There they immediately recognized that Jesus is real and gave their lives to Him as Lord and Savior.

Can you imagine the joy of that missionary and of all who prayed with Him? The Holy Spirit who led that man to Africa was the one who moved through his prayers to touch his parents. The Spirit is not limited by time and space; He's not confined or restricted in any way. *Where we are not, He is.* And He is working.

FREEDOM AS NEVER BEFORE

There comes a point in your life when the Lord opens your eyes to understand what the Christian life was meant to be. It isn't just going to heaven when you die; it's dying to self on earth and allowing Him to live through you.

Once that's clear in your heart, once you've chosen to release everything to Him, then you'll know freedom like never before. The burden of service dissipates, and the Spirit will carry you into the Father's perfect will. In that place you'll experience the mighty power of God. There are no more excuses for inactivity; there is no more justification for shallow character. There's only the Lord and our willingness to trust Him and respond to the Holy Spirit.

So the question comes to each of us: *Who is the Holy Spirit to me?* What have I done with Him? Or perhaps better expressed, What has He done with me?

Have you neglected God's gift of the Holy Spirit who has taken up residence in your life? Are you content to hear stories of great men and women of the past, or do you want God to use *you*?

If you want Him to use you, it's just a prayer away. This isn't a complicated thing. Just pray and ask God to fill you with His Spirit.

As you've been reading, the Holy Spirit has been testifying to your spirit that you need to release your life to Him. Yield yourself as He begins to work in and through your life to accomplish the Father's will.

COME TO JESUS

The first requirement of walking with Jesus is to "come." Jesus doesn't primarily say to us, "Do this," or, "Don't do that." He says, *"Come to Me."* We often would rather go and do something *for* Him than simply come *to* Him. For we're not sure we want to be where He is or hear what He might say. We would rather be doing something that's on our own hearts and aren't always interested in what's on His heart. But He is the Master and we are the servants. When He says come, we must come.

That may seem simple and obvious, but it's a huge barrier for many people. Our Lord has said, "I have come that you might have abundant life, so come and receive it! There's nothing too big for Me, and nothing's too small for Me." But He doesn't dispense abundant life like medicine; it's found *in Him.* You don't drop by and get a quick fix; rest for your soul is found *in His presence.* As long as you remain in Him, He'll bring that soul-rest, but you have to start by simply coming to Jesus.

We've discovered that there are primarily two categories of people—not the intellectual and the simple, but the willing and the unwilling. You must be willing to come; that's the first step you must take if you want to experience God's power in your life.

WHO'S IN CHARGE?

I (Mel) met with a doctor who was struggling to release control of his life and come to Jesus. He's a man used to being in charge. He worked in emergency medicine and made his living by directing the actions of others and making the tough decisions. He had a beautiful family, a nice home, and a strong career, and he was unwilling to turn things over to anybody else, including God.

Finally he said to me, "I like to be in charge; it's just how I'm made."

"That isn't true," I challenged him. "*God* made you! And He made you for a relationship with Himself. Anything that hinders that relationship is sin. But when the problem is sin, there's a solution: Jesus came to save you from your sin."

"I guess I don't have any excuse then, do I?" he responded.

"None that God cannot deal with," I said. That night he decided to put his life in God's hands. For the first time, he was *willing* to following Jesus.

Are you willing to come to Jesus? That's where it all begins. That's the first step in experiencing the power of the Holy Spirit in your life.

The Spirit Is Speaking...

As you meditate upon the message you've heard in this book, has the Holy Spirit impressed upon you truth that requires a response? You've considered the message of God's Word, and now you must decide whether you believe it. You've heard the testimony of those who have learned to walk in the Spirit, but now you must choose if you want to experience Him in your life. The truth must move from your head to your heart if it's to transform your life.

Is the Holy Spirit moving you out of your comfort zone and into the Father's will? "Without faith it is impossible to please Him" (Hebrews 11:6). Are you doing anything that requires faith? Are you living in the power of the Holy Spirit, a power that's beyond your natural abilities?

Perhaps you need to ask the Spirit to guide you in an appropriate response.

DECIDE TO RECEIVE

To know the heart of God for your life is more than good news; it's an opportunity to experience abundant life. If you're to receive the gift of the Holy Spirit in your life and live in His presence, you must make a decision. It's a decision to receive Him by faith.

There are three distinct steps to receiving, by faith, the promise of the Holy Spirit.

First, you must *repent*. Peter said in Acts 2:38, "Repent, and let every one of you be baptized in the name of Jesus Christ for the remission of sins; and you shall receive the gift of the Holy Spirit." You may have disregarded this statement as one given to sinners, those who haven't yet put their trust in Jesus. But that's not true. It's for everyone—the Christian as well as the non-Christian. If you want to know the presence of the Holy Spirit, you must live a life of repentance. As soon as conviction comes, repent. Turn from your sin and find forgiveness and cleansing in the blood of Christ.

As soon as people cry out for a filling of the Spirit, there will immediately be conviction of sin. They'll be convicted not only of God's laws, which they have broken, but of the spiritual apathy that has left them weak and powerless. They'll acknowledge their desperate condition and seek forgiveness for neglecting the Spirit in their lives. Everything must be surrendered into the hands of the living God if you want to know His presence fresh and anew. For until you're cleansed of sin, you won't know the power of Pentecost.

Second, you must *ask*. This sounds almost too simple, yet it's so very necessary if you want to know the power of the Holy Spirit. You have not because you ask not (see James 4:2). You must specifically and intentionally ask God to fill you with His Spirit.

Consider this: If God were to respond in proportion to your asking, would He sense your desperate need of the Holy Spirit? Would He conclude that you couldn't live without His life within? Would He be convinced you want to live the Spirit-filled life? Then start asking.

Hear again the wonderful promise of our Lord: "If you then, being evil, know how to give good gifts to your children, how much more will your heavenly Father give the Holy Spirit to those who ask Him!" (Luke 11:13). Do you believe your heavenly Father wants to give you the Holy Spirit in all His fullness? Then ask Him.

Third, if you want to experience the Holy Spirit in your life, you must *receive* Him. You must make room for Him in your life and start living under His influence. Claim by faith the promise of God. Stop making excuses, and be who God called you to be.

Live in constant fellowship with the Spirit, and obey everything He says. Don't worry about tomorrow; respond to Him today. You'll discover that every step of obedience leads to a greater experience with Him. And someday, you'll look back on your life and be absolutely amazed by what God has done both in you and through you.

LOOK FOR THE HUNGRY

One last word as you begin this journey: Look for others who are hungry for a fresh touch of the Spirit. Bind your life together with others, and cry out to God. Don't be a maverick who desires a special anointing, but humbly pray for one another in the body of Christ.

When you find others who long to be filled with the Spirit, you're well on your way to seeing Him move in power. For He is the one who has placed it in your heart. He is the one working in those around you. As you join together, there's power in corporate prayer. That's God's pattern. The working of the Spirit is like leaven: though it may start out small, it will grow. And if He's working in your life, it's for the purpose of bringing a blessing to the entire body.

Are you willing to pay the price to be filled with the Spirit? Are you one through whom God will bring revival to the land? The gift of the Spirit is not for the great, but for every believer who would take God at His word. What you do next reveals what you believe about God.

Experiencing the Spirit

Chapter 1—Revealing the Unknowable

1. How would you summarize your present understanding of who the Holy Spirit is? What has been your experience with the Holy Spirit?

2. As we seek to better understand the Holy Spirit's ministry to our lives, why is it important to fully realize the damage and spiritual blindness caused by sin?

3. In our coming to God and forming a relationship with Him, what is God's part, and what is our part?

4. What are your answers to the following questions from this chapter's text: *Have you gone beyond accepting the fact that there's a God? Have you moved beyond accepting Christ as God's Son and made Him Lord of your life?*

5. Why do you think so many Christians fail to experience the depths of what God has purposed for their lives?

6. Look again at what Jesus says in Matthew 12:31–32. Why is blasphemy against the Holy Spirit so serious?

7. How is the Holy Spirit like the wind in the sails of a ship? How does that relate to your own life?

8. Quietly review what you have learned through reading this chapter and from your study. What are the most significant things God's Spirit is saying to you at this time? What are the things you know God wants you to do (or keep doing)

in response to this encounter with Him? What adjustments does He want you to make?

CHAPTER 2—THE EVER-PRESENT GOD

1. How open have your eyes been to God's work all around you? How much of His work do you think you are recognizing?
2. Look closely again at the words of Jesus in John 5:19–20. To what extent does this passage relate to your own life?
3. Why is recognizing God's activity so critically important when it comes to the spiritual warfare we face?
4. What names for God carry special significance for you in your own experience with Him?
5. How have you recognized the Holy Spirit's ministry in your life in opening your eyes to what God is doing and giving you the ability to respond to it?
6. In your own experience, what has it meant for God to pour out His Holy Spirit?
7. Quietly review what you have learned through reading this chapter and from your study. What are the most significant things God's Spirit is saying to you at this time? What are the things that you know God wants you to do (or keep doing) in response to this encounter with Him? What adjustments does He want you to make?

CHAPTER 3—GIFTED TO SERVE

1. As you've read about the life of Jesus in the gospels, what stands out most to you? What kind of information about Jesus do you see the gospel writers emphasizing?

2. How would you describe the humility of Jesus? How was it demonstrated?

3. How and why was Jesus forced to rely upon the Holy Spirit as His source of wisdom and power?

4. In His life on earth, how was Christ's experience of the Spirit also meant to be like yours?

5. What most convinces you that God understands and sympathizes with your pain and troubles? How does this help you?

6. What are God's most meaningful promises to you concerning the Holy Spirit's presence?

7. As you contemplate the theme of this chapter, how is Jesus' life of humility an example to us of being "gifted to serve"?

8. Quietly review what you have learned through reading this chapter and from your study. What are the most significant things God's Spirit is saying to you at this time? What are the things that you know God wants you to do (or keep doing) in response to this encounter with Him? What adjustments does He want you to make?

CHAPTER 4—HIS GIFT TO GIVE

1. At what point in Jesus' life and ministry on earth did He begin to teach His disciples extensively about the Holy Spirit? Why did He wait until then?

2. In chapters 14–16 of John's gospel, what significant things did Jesus teach His disciples about the Holy Spirit? (Take time to thoroughly explore these chapters.)

3. Why is it necessary for us to obey Christ as Lord before we receive enabling power from the Holy Spirit?

4. What is the meaning of being baptized "with the Holy Spirit and fire" (Luke 3:16)? How have you personally experienced this?

5. What is the "chaff" in your life that the Spirit has had to winnow out?

6. What is the practical difference between (a) thinking that we're sent out as witnesses *for* Christ and (b) thinking that we're sent out *with* Christ as a witness to Him? What makes this difference significant?

7. Quietly review what you have learned through reading this chapter and from your study. What are the most significant things God's Spirit is saying to you at this time? What are the things that you know God wants you to do (or keep doing) in response to this encounter with Him? What adjustments does He want you to make?

CHAPTER 5—THE GIFT OF RELATIONSHIP

1. Think about your own longings and efforts to discover your part in the work of God's kingdom. Do your thoughts and questions in this area tend to be more self-centered or more God-centered? Explain your answer.

2. What difference do you think it makes in our relationship with God when we discover that our natural talents, abilities, and skills are different from spiritual gifts given by the Holy Spirit?

3. A personal relationship implies many things—all built on the foundation of a solid awareness and understanding of the other person. Think about your current understanding of the Holy Spirit and what He means to you. How do you currently experience His presence? And what do you personally want most to learn about Him?

4. According to God's promise in each of the following passages, what exactly are we meant to experience because of the Holy Spirit?

John 7:38–39
John 16:13–15
Romans 8:11
Romans 8:15–16
Romans 8:26–27

5. As you seek to obey the Lord and live the kind of life He has called you to, what areas of need or weakness or inadequacy do you most frequently recognize and think about? And how have they limited your service to God?

6. At this point, what is your understanding of how God's Holy Spirit wants to operate in your life to provide His fullness and power in areas of perceived need? Also, how do you think He wants to work in areas of your natural strengths?

7. Acts 2:38–39 is a foundational scripture for believers to build upon. Listen again to the apostle Peter's words to the people on the Day of Pentecost: "Repent, and let every one of you be baptized in the name of Jesus Christ for the remis-sion of sins; and you shall receive the gift of the Holy Spirit. For the promise is to you and to your children, and to all who are afar off, as many as the Lord our God will call." According to this passage, what is the spiritual gift that believers in Jesus Christ receive? And why is it so important for us to always remember this? What practical difference would it make in your life to fully grasp this truth and consistently maintain this perspective?

8. All people on earth have gifts, but only Christians have spiritual gifts. The distinction is significant. What are the most important things in your life which you are already fully convinced that the Holy Spirit has provided you? (Take time right now to thank Him again for these things.)

9. What does it really mean to walk in the Spirit's fullness and power? In your own life, how are you pursuing this?

10. Think carefully about each phrase in Paul's profound statement in 1 Corinthians 12:7: "[a] The manifestation of the Spirit... [b] is given to each one... [c] for the profit of all." How does each phrase relate to your own life and your own relationship to the Holy Spirit?

11. In what particular ways do you believe God has called you at this time to share your life with His people and serve them in order to help build up His church?

12. Quietly review what you have learned through reading this chapter and from your study. What are the most significant things God's Spirit is saying to you at this time? What are the things that you know God wants you to do (or keep doing) in response to this encounter with Him? What adjustments does He want you to make?

CHAPTER 6—SHAPED FOR SERVICE

1. How much have you struggled with thinking that God cannot use you? What reasons for this were in your mind?

2. What purposes on God's heart have you sensed that He wants you to be a part of?

3. What assignments has God already given you? What did they mean in your relationship with Him?

4. What assignment from God are you currently working on? How is it deepening your relationship with Him?

5. Think again of what is taught about Jesus in Hebrews 5:8: "He learned obedience by the things which He suffered." What does this statement imply about *your* life? What will it mean for the Holy Spirit to make you Christlike? What must the Holy Spirit do to build great character in you?

6. Are you willing for the Holy Spirit to build great character into your life? Are you willing no matter how much suffering and hardship it brings?

7. How has God used other believers to strengthen and encourage you as you went through challenging times?

8. Who are the Christians who are regularly praying for you now? Why are their prayers so important and valuable?

9. Quietly review what you have learned through reading this chapter and from your study. What are the most significant things God's Spirit is saying to you at this time? What are the things that you know God wants you to do (or keep doing) in response to this encounter with Him? What adjustments does He want you to make?

CHAPTER 7—GOD'S BEST IN YOUR LIFE

1. At this point in your understanding, are you fully convinced there's a significant difference between a spiritual gift

and a natural talent or ability that God gives? If so, how would you describe this difference? And how would you be able to detect it in your own life as well as in the lives of others you observe?

2. To what degree, if any, have you considered serving God outside your areas of strength and proficiency? Can you imagine God asking you to do that which you don't like to do?

3. What has been your experience, if any, with spiritual gift assessments or inventories? If you've taken one, what did it reveal about you? How would you assess the test's ability to discover what the Holy Spirit wants to do in and through your life, as compared with its ability to identify your natural strengths?

4. To what extent do you agree that the results of a spiritual gift inventory test should not be used as a guide for how God desires to use you in the future? Why or why not?

5. Review again Paul's foundational teaching on spiritual gifts in 1 Corinthians 12:1–11. What relevant principles and guidelines do you see in this passage that help us most in evaluating and determining our spiritual gifts?

6. When outsiders look at your church, do they see the power of God working through His people to accomplish what only He can do?

7. Notice the descriptions of the early church in Acts 2:42–47 (after the Holy Spirit came at Pentecost) and in Acts

4:31–35 (following a time of being filled by the Spirit).
What do you see as the most important lessons we can learn
today from these passages about dependence on the Spirit?

8. To what extent are you tempted to rely on your abilities
and talents rather than the power of the Holy Spirit? Has
this been a problem for you in the past? Is it a danger now?

9. Can you identify any "limits" that you've imposed on God's
use of your life? If so, talk with God about them.

10. What are some potentially difficult or uncomfortable
assignments that God might possibly be calling you to and
to which you must be open?

11. Look carefully at what Peter wrote about our spiritual gifts
in this passage: "As each one has received a gift, minister it
to one another, as good stewards of the manifold grace of
God. If anyone speaks, let him speak as the oracles of God.
If anyone ministers, let him do it as with the ability which
God supplies, that in all things God may be glorified
through Jesus Christ, to whom belong the glory and the
dominion forever and ever" (1 Peter 4:10–11). What over-
arching purpose for the use of our gifts did Peter teach here,
and what does this mean for you in practical terms?

12. From each of the following passages, summarize what the
Holy Spirit guided Jesus to do in His life on earth. Then
tell in what way, if any, this might relate with what you
know God wants you to do in your life.

Matthew 12:28
Luke 4:1
Luke 4:14–16
Luke 4:18–19
Acts 10:38

13. Why did Jesus need the Holy Spirit's power as He followed His Father's will in His ministry?

14. Quietly review what you have learned through reading this chapter and from your study. What are the most significant things God's Spirit is saying to you at this time? What are the things that you know God wants you to do (or keep doing) in response to this encounter with Him? What adjustments does He want you to make?

CHAPTER 8—TALENTED OR GIFTED?

1. Look closely at each of the following passages. What does it teach us about those whom God chooses and why He chooses them?
   Deuteronomy 7:7–9
   Matthew 11:25–26
   1 Corinthians 1:26–29
   James 2:5

2. In 2 Chronicles 16:9, one of the Lord's prophets speaks these words to the king of Judah: "For the eyes of the LORD

run to and fro throughout the whole earth, to show Himself strong on behalf of those whose heart is loyal to Him." Other versions render this last phrase as "blameless toward him" (ESV), "fully committed to him" (NIV), and "completely His" (NASB). What does such a heart toward God mean to you personally? How would you describe it in your own words? What is it that makes possible such a loyal, obedient heart within you?

3. What strong encouragement for a better heart do you find in each of the following passages?
   2 Corinthians 4:6
   2 Thessalonians 3:5
   Hebrews 10:22–23

4. What examples from Scripture can you recall of ordinary people who were gifted and equipped by God to do something far outside the "normal" range of their abilities?

5. What man or woman in the Bible do you most look up to as an ordinary person whom God chose and gifted? In what ways can you most identify with this "hero"? What was most important in this person's life—relationship or talents?

6. In Paul's discussion in Romans 12:3–8, notice how he brought together the dynamics of humility, faith, and our active use of spiritual gifts. How does this passage relate most to what you've been learning about spiritual gifted-

ness? And what encouragement and help do you find here for your own life?

7. Acts 8:9–24 tells the story of a new believer who wanted to obtain a spiritual gift in the wrong way. What do you think are the most important lessons for us to learn from this incident?

8. In regard to the spiritual gifts we may seek, what conclusions did Paul come to in 1 Corinthians 12:27–13:3? How do you think this applies to your life at this time?

9. Quietly review what you have learned through reading this chapter and from your study. What are the most significant things God's Spirit is saying to you at this time? What are the things that you know God wants you to do (or keep doing) in response to this encounter with Him? What adjustments does He want you to make?

Chapter 9—From Ordinary to Extraordinary

1. Why is it so important to remember that equipping *follows* our assignments from God rather than precedes them?

2. Think objectively and in a fresh way about these words of Jesus: "All authority has been given to Me in heaven and on earth. Go therefore and make disciples of all the nations, baptizing them in the name of the Father and of the Son

and of the Holy Spirit, teaching them to observe all things that I have commanded you; and lo, I am with you always, even to the end of the age" (Matthew 28:18–20). How do His words convince you that He wants you involved in His work to redeem this world?

3. Reflect in the same way on these words of Jesus: "You did not choose Me, but I chose you and appointed you that you should go and bear fruit, and that your fruit should remain, that whatever you ask the Father in My name He may give you" (John 15:16). Again, how do these words convince you that your Savior wants you involved in His work to redeem this world?

4. What is the Holy Spirit doing right now to bring your life into harmony with His activity so that He can accomplish His work through you?

5. What would you say are the most important things you've seen God do in your past as they relate to what He may want you to do now and in the future?

6. What particular abilities, skills, and talents do you possess as a result of what God has done for you in the past?

7. What exactly has God called you to invest your life in?

8. What are the ministries that have captured your heart?

9. Is the Lord using your life in such a way that you sense God's pleasure?

10. What tasks do you face that require the work of the Holy Spirit in order for you to accomplish them?

11. What is there in your life right now to indicate that you trust in the Lord?

12. How confident can you be in the Holy Spirit's personal guidance for you? And how can you pray effectively for His guidance? Read the following passages reflectively, and record your thoughts on each one:

    Psalm 143:10
    John 16:13–15
    Romans 8:14
    Colossians 1:9–10

13. Are you ready for God to reveal His assignment in your life? *Any* assignment? Are you prepared to say yes before you know what He'll ask?

14. Read Luke 10:1–12, where Jesus sends out a large group of His followers in ministry. How would you summarize their assignment?

15. In Luke 10:17, what results did these disciples report when they returned?

16. In Luke 10:19, what did Jesus say He had given to these disciples so they could fulfill their assignment?

17. In Luke 10:21–24, what is most significant to you about the way Jesus responded to the ministry of these disciples?

18. Quietly review what you have learned through reading this chapter and from your study. What are the most significant things God's Spirit is saying to you at this time? What are the things that you know God wants you to do (or keep doing) in response to this encounter with Him? What adjustments does He want you to make?

Chapter 10—Keeping the Relationship Alive

1. What appropriate response to God and His work in our lives is taught in Philippians 2:12–13? How does this passage relate to your own response to God in this season of your life?

2. What wrong response to the Spirit did Paul mention in Ephesians 4:30–31? How would you describe this kind of response in your own words?

3. In what way might you have recently grieved the Holy Spirit? If the Lord brings something to mind, use this as an opportunity for confession before Him.

4. What wrong response to the Spirit is mentioned by Stephen in Acts 7:51? How would you describe it in your own words?

5. You may be particularly inclined to a certain way of resisting the Holy Spirit. If so, what is it? The degree to which we resist the Holy Spirit is the degree to which we prevent

Him from working through us. If the Lord brings something to mind, use this opportunity to confess it to Him.

6. Jesus said, "Most assuredly, I say to you, he who receives whomever I send receives Me; and he who receives Me receives Him who sent Me" (John 13:20). How do these words apply to situations in which we resist the Spirit's message as it comes through other people?

7. If you want the Holy Spirit to speak to your heart, you must let Him speak through any means He chooses. In what circumstances are you most likely to resist something that the Spirit might be telling you through others? Who are the people with whom your resistance is more likely to happen? Again, if the Lord brings some people to mind, use this opportunity to confess this to Him, and ask for His help in overcoming this resistance in the future.

8. What wrong response to the Spirit is mentioned in 1 Thessalonians 5:19? How would you describe this response in your own words?

9. Have you witnessed someone quench the Spirit's work? In what way might you have recently quenched His work? Once more, if the Lord brings something to mind, use this as an opportunity for confession before Him.

10. The good news is that *in Christ* we are free to not quench or resist or grieve the Spirit. Why is this good news true, according to your own understanding of what Jesus Christ

has done for us? (You may want to look especially at passages such as Romans 6:4–14; 6:22; and 8:5–14.)

11. What correct response to the Spirit did Paul teach in Ephesians 5:18? How would you describe this response in your
own words? What did Paul mean?

12. According to Galatians 5:16–25, as you allow the Spirit to
fill you and as you walk in His presence, what can you
expect Him to do for you? (Think of this especially in
terms of your everyday life, and the specific circumstances
and responsibilities that are now yours.)

13. What else besides time does the building of godly character
take, according to your understanding of the Scriptures?

14. Quietly review what you have learned through reading this
chapter and from your study. What are the most significant
things God's Spirit is saying to you at this time? What are
the things that you know God wants you to do (or keep
doing) in response to this encounter with Him? What
adjustments does He want you to make?

CHAPTER 11—A LIFE FILLED TO THE FULL

1. What do you anticipate life in the Spirit to look like in your
future? What are your expectations, especially in terms of
the fulfillment and joy you hope to experience and the kind
of service among God's people that He will lead you into?

2. What degree of inner satisfaction did Jesus discuss in John 4:14 and John 7:37–39? How would you relate these words of Jesus to your own experience?

3. Think deeply about Jesus' invitation in John 7:37—"Come to Me and drink." Take a moment to praise and thank Jesus Christ for how He wants to fill you and for what this reveals about His heart and His character.

4. Regarding your attitudes toward sin and self, what relevant truths for your life do you find in the following passages? How does each one especially concern your life at this time?
Ephesians 4:17–24
Colossians 3:1–17

5. How is a hunger to know Christ demonstrated in each of the following verses? How is each statement a standard for your own spiritual hunger?
Philippians 1:21
Philippians 3:8–10

6. When it comes to our spiritual gifts, what purpose for them did Paul teach us to strive for in 1 Corinthians 14:12? And what does this mean to you in practical terms?

7. In 1 Timothy 4:14, what did Paul tell Timothy *not* to do with his spiritual gift? In your own life, how can you avoid making this mistake that Paul warned Timothy not to make?

8. Quietly review what you have learned through reading this chapter and from your study. What are the most significant

things God's Spirit is saying to you at this time? What are the things that you know God wants you to do (or keep doing) in response to this encounter with Him? What adjustments does He want you to make?

CHAPTER 12—COMPLETE SURRENDER

1. How have you already discovered the *uniqueness* of your relationship with God? In what ways do you see the personal nature of your relationship with Him?

2. Have you made the deliberate decision to allow the Holy Spirit to have complete access to your life? Describe that moment or explain why not.

3. Do you generally make decisions based upon your ability to achieve results, or upon the Spirit's leading and equipping? Explain.

4. Read John 20:19–23 and think about what Jesus did for His disciples on the evening following His resurrection. How would you describe the significance of this event for those men—and for us?

5. What most convinces you that you are alive at this moment in history because of a mission from Jesus—because He is sending you?

6. Looking at the lives of the disciples and the early believers

who followed, what do you honestly expect your own mission from Jesus to cost you?

7. As you follow the Lord in obedience in the assignments He has for your life, what are you convinced that you can rely on the Holy Spirit for?

8. Explore God's heart and His promises for His people in each of the following passages:

Jeremiah 33:2–3

Jeremiah 32:17

Romans 8:31

9. Take a moment to express to the Lord your faith and confidence in Him as you consider the Holy Spirit's desire to guide and empower you in His assignments.

10. How would you answer these questions: *Who is the Holy Spirit to me? What have I done with Him? What has He done with me?*

11. Quietly review what you have learned through your reading and study in this book. What are the most significant things God's Spirit is saying to you? What are the things that you know God wants you to do (or keep doing) in response to your encounter with Him at this time? What adjustments does He want you to make?

FOR FURTHER STUDY, REFLECTION, AND APPLICATION

You may sense that God wants to speak more to you from His Word about certain aspects of what you've studied and read about in this book. Review carefully and prayerfully the following list of topics. As you are led by the Spirit, open up the Scriptures to any of the listed passages, and allow Him to speak to you. As you do this, make a written note of your thoughts.

The demonstration of God's power in our lives
> Romans 15:13
> Romans 15:18–19
> 1 Corinthians 2:3–5
> 1 Corinthians 4:20
> 1 Thessalonians 1:5

God-centered living and thinking
> Proverbs 3:5–6
> Isaiah 8:13
> Mark 12:30
> Colossians 3:17

The importance of an intimate relationship with the Lord
> John 14:7
> John 14:16–21
> 1 Corinthians 8:3
> 1 John 3:1–3

Recognizing our neediness
> Psalm 40:17
> 1 Corinthians 4:7
> Philippians 4:11–13

The Spirit is the gift
 Luke 11:13
 Acts 5:31–32
 Acts 11:11–18
 Romans 5:5
 1 Corinthians 3:16–17
 2 Corinthians 5:5
 Galatians 4:6–7
 Titus 3:5–6
 1 John 4:13

In the Spirit we find everything we need
 John 14:26
 1 Corinthians 2:9–16
 2 Corinthians 1:20–22
 Galatians 5:22–23
 Ephesians 1:3
 Ephesians 1:13–14
 1 John 2:20

Walking in the Spirit's fullness and power
 Mark 13:11
 Luke 3:16
 Acts 1:8
 Galatians 5:16–18

 Ephesians 3:16
 Ephesians 5:18–21

Our gifts in the Spirit are for serving God's people
 1 Corinthians 12:12–13
 Galatians 5:13
 Ephesians 2:22
 Philippians 2:1–2
 Colossians 1:8
 1 Thessalonians 4:9

Spiritual gifts and natural talents and abilities
 1 Corinthians 14:1
 1 Corinthians 14:12
 Galatians 6:7–9
 1 Timothy 4:14

Reliance on the Holy Spirit versus self-reliance
 John 6:63
 John 15:26
 Romans 8:5–6
 Romans 8:13
 Philippians 3:3
 1 John 4:1–2

Called to do the impossible
 2 Corinthians 6:4–10
 2 Timothy 1:8
 Hebrews 10:35–36

Obedience in difficult assignments
 Luke 1:38
 Acts 26:15–23
 2 Timothy 2:3–7
 Hebrews 11:32–40

Limiting God's work
 Isaiah 59:1–2
 Mark 6:5–6
 Mark 9:23

God gets the glory
 Romans 4:20–21
 Romans 11:36
 Romans 15:7
 Ephesians 3:20–21
 Philippians 1:9–11
 Philippians 4:19–20
 1 Timothy 1:17
 1 Peter 4:14

The source of Jesus' power
 Isaiah 11:1–5

 Isaiah 42:1
 Isaiah 61:1–3
 Matthew 4:1
 John 1:32–34
 John 3:34
 Acts 1:2
 Hebrews 1:8–9
 Hebrews 9:14

The life of Jesus as our example
 John 13:15
 1 Corinthians 11:1
 Ephesians 5:1–2
 1 Peter 2:21
 1 John 2:6

True humility
 Psalm 10:17
 Psalm 25:9
 Romans 12:16
 Ephesians 4:2–4
 James 3:17

Being chosen by God
 Matthew 22:14
 2 Thessalonians 2:13–15
 James 2:5
 1 Peter 2:4–5

The right heart
: 1 Chronicles 28:9
: Psalm 51:10
: Psalm 119:2
: Ezekiel 36:26–27
: Hebrews 4:12
: Hebrews 10:22

God uses very ordinary people
: Matthew 11:25
: 1 Corinthians 1:20
: 1 Corinthians 2:1–5
: James 2:5

Walking in the Spirit
: Luke 2:25–32
: Romans 8:2–4
: Galatians 5:25
: Ephesians 6:17
: Colossians 3:16
: 2 Timothy 1:14

Equipping follows assignment
: Exodus 31:1–5
: Judges 14:5–6
: Judges 15:14–15
: 2 Chronicles 20:1–15

Ezekiel 2:1–2
Ezekiel 3:22–24
Micah 3:8
Acts 6:3–6

God is at work and invites us to join Him
: John 5:17
: John 5:19–20
: 1 Corinthians 12:6
: Colossians 1:28–29

Remembering God's work in our past
: Psalm 103:1–5
: Psalm 105:5
: Psalm 143:5
: Luke 1:49
: Romans 11:22

God's personal calling for us
: Matthew 28:19
: Mark 10:49–52
: 2 Corinthians 3:18
: Ephesians 2:19
: 1 Thessalonians 4:7
: Hebrews 13:20–21
: 1 Peter 1:15–19

Knowing Christ well
    John 6:66–69
    Ephesians 1:17
    Ephesians 3:17–19
    2 Timothy 1:12
    2 Peter 3:18

Trusting the Lord's guidance
    Isaiah 30:21
    Acts 13:1–4
    Acts 16:6–10
    Acts 19:21

Heart surrender
    Matthew 11:28–30
    2 Corinthians 7:1
    Ephesians 5:20–21
    Hebrews 3:12–15
    James 4:6–8

Sin that grieves the Spirit
    Psalm 51:3–11
    Isaiah 63:10
    1 Corinthians 6:18–20

Sin that resists the Spirit
    Nehemiah 9:29
    Psalm 106:33

    Acts 5:1–11
    1 Thessalonians 4:7–8
    2 Timothy 3:8

God speaks through others
    Acts 11:27–28
    Acts 21:4
    Acts 21:8–14

Sin that quenches the Spirit
    Nehemiah 9:29
    Isaiah 30:1

Sin's consequences
    John 8:34
    Galatians 6:8
    James 1:14–16

Freedom not to sin
    Jeremiah 24:7
    Romans 8:2
    1 Corinthians 6:11

Being filled with the Spirit
    John 14:16–17
    Acts 7:55–56
    Acts 13:52
    2 Corinthians 13:14

Colossians 1:9
1 Peter 4:14

Our character
Matthew 13:23
Romans 5:3–5
Philippians 4:8
1 Thessalonians 2:12
2 Peter 1:5–9

The adventure of obedience
Ezekiel 37:1–14
Acts 8:26–39
Acts 9:31
1 John 2:3–6
1 John 2:17

Satisfaction with Christ
Psalm 36:7–8
Psalm 73:25–26
Luke 10:38–42

Dissatisfaction with self
Job 42:5–6
Ezekiel 36:31
1 Timothy 1:15

Hunger to know Christ more
Psalm 42:1
Psalm 143:6
Isaiah 26:8–9
Hebrews 12:2–3

Love for God's people
Colossians 3:12–17
1 Peter 1:22
1 John 3:14
1 John 4:19–21

Continual openness to the Spirit's work
Galatians 3:2–3
Galatians 5:25
1 Timothy 4:12
Revelation 2:7

The privilege of being used in God's kingdom work
Acts 20:22–24
2 Corinthians 3:3–6
2 Corinthians 5:16–21

Counting the cost
Luke 14:25–33
Luke 18:22–30
Philippians 3:7

Freedom in the Spirit
    Isaiah 55:12
    Romans 7:5–6
    Romans 14:17–18
    2 Corinthians 3:17
    Philippians 1:19
    1 Thessalonians 1:6
    Jude 20–21

Life with God was Meant to be Experienced
It Starts Here

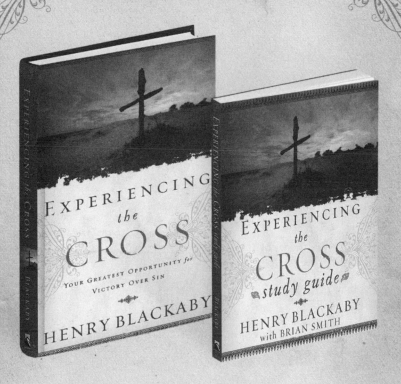

Henry Blackaby leads you on an exploration through the deeper dimensions of the cross, ensuring that the further you go, the more you will: Deal radically and completely with sin, embrace true and lasting union with Christ, and experience the fullness and reality of His victory in your life. Will you yield to God's provision in His cross? Will you receive the power and presence of Jesus Christ? Will you dare to experience the cross? Study Guide Also Available.

Go Further with Your Experience

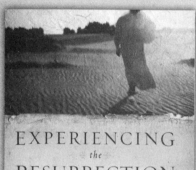
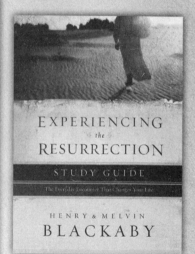

EXPERIENCING
the
RESURRECTION

The EVERYDAY ENCOUNTER
That CHANGES *Your* LIFE!

HENRY & MEL
BLACKABY

EXPERIENCING
the
RESURRECTION

STUDY GUIDE

The Everyday Encounter That Changes Your Life

HENRY & MELVIN
BLACKABY

This book invites you to experience the living Christ in your life...day by day and moment by moment. First you'll explore the meaning and purpose of the resurrection in the mind of God. Then you'll witness it in the life of the Lord Jesus. And finally you'll experience personally the peace, joy, power, authority, confidence, and hope the resurrection can generate in your life.